Maya Angelou

by Gail B. Stewart

LUCENT BOOKS

A part of Gale, Cengage Learning

GALE
CENGAGE Learning

Detroit • New York • San Francisco • New Haven, Conn • Waterville, Maine • London

GALE
CENGAGE Learning™

LIBRARY OF CONGRESS CATALOGING-IN-PUBLICATION DATA

Stewart, Gail B. (Gail Barbara), 1949–
Maya Angelou / by Gail B. Stewart.
  p. cm. — (People in the news)
Includes bibliographical references and index.
ISBN 978-1-4205-0092-9
1. Angelou, Maya—Juvenile literature. 2. Authors, American—20th century—Biography—Juvenile literature. 3. African American women civil rights workers—United States—Biography—Juvenile literature. 4. African American authors—Biography—Juvenile literature. I. Title.
  PS3551.N464Z92 2009
  818'.5409—dc22
  [B]
                                                    2008048912

Lucent Books
27500 Drake Rd.
Farmington Hills, MI 48331

ISBN-13: 978-1-4205-0092-9
ISBN-10: 1-4205-0092-9

Printed in the United States of America
1 2 3 4 5 6 7 13 12 11 10 09

Contents

F ame and celebrity are alluring. People are drawn to those who walk in fame's spotlight, whether they are known for great accomplishments or for notorious deeds. The lives of the famous pique public interest and attract attention, perhaps because their experiences seem in some ways so different from, yet in other ways so similar to, our own.

Newspapers, magazines, and television regularly capitalize on this fascination with celebrity by running profiles of famous people. For example, television programs such as *Entertainment Tonight* devote all of their programming to stories about entertainment and entertainers. Magazines such as *People* fill their pages with stories of the private lives of famous people. Even newspapers, newsmagazines, and television news frequently delve into the lives of well-known personalities. Despite the number of articles and programs, few provide more than a superficial glimpse at their subjects.

Lucent's People in the News series offers young readers a deeper look into the lives of today's newsmakers, the influences that have shaped them, and the impact they have had in their fields of endeavor and on other people's lives. The subjects of the series hail from many disciplines and walks of life. They include authors, musicians, athletes, political leaders, entertainers, entrepreneurs, and others who have made a mark on modern life and who, in many cases, will continue to do so for years to come.

These biographies are more than factual chronicles. Each book emphasizes the contributions, accomplishments, or deeds that have brought fame or notoriety to the individual and shows how that person has influenced modern life. Authors portray their subjects in a realistic, unsentimental light. For example, Bill Gates—the cofounder and chief executive officer of the software giant Microsoft—has been instrumental in making personal computers the most vital tool of the modern age. Few dispute his business savvy, his perseverance, or his technical expertise, yet critics say he is ruthless in his dealings with competitors and driven more by his desire to maintain Microsoft's dominance in the computer industry than by an interest in furthering technology.

In these books, young readers will encounter inspiring stories about real people who achieved success despite enormous obstacles. Oprah Winfrey—the most powerful, most watched, and wealthiest woman on television today—spent the first six years of her life in the care of her grandparents while her unwed mother sought work and a better life elsewhere. Her adolescence was colored by promiscuity, pregnancy at age fourteen, rape, and sexual abuse.

Each author documents and supports his or her work with an array of primary and secondary source quotations taken from diaries, letters, speeches, and interviews. All quotes are footnoted to show readers exactly how and where biographers derive their information and provide guidance for further research. The quotations enliven the text by giving readers eyewitness views of the life and accomplishments of each person covered in the People in the News series.

In addition, each book in the series includes photographs, annotated bibliographies, timelines, and comprehensive indexes. For both the casual reader and the student researcher, the People in the News series offers insight into the lives of today's newsmakers—people who shape the way we live, work, and play in the modern age.

A Terrifying Honor

Just days after Bill Clinton was elected president of the United States in 1992, Maya Angelou received an unusual request. Clinton was an admirer of her writing—especially her poetry. He wanted to know if she would be willing to write a poem for his inauguration in January and read it at the ceremony.

"I Was Flabbergasted"

The reading of a poem at a presidential inauguration was somewhat unusual in the United States. In fact, not since Robert Frost read a special poem at John F. Kennedy's swearing-in ceremony in 1961 had a poet been invited to participate at an inauguration.

It was an honor, of course—especially for Angelou. Never had a woman or an African American poet been invited to read at an inauguration—and Maya Angelou fit into both of those categories.

Weeks later, Angelou recalled her reaction to being chosen to write an inaugural poem:

> I thought of my grandmother . . . and my grandfather . . . and my great-grandmother who had been born a slave in Arkansas. I thought, how would those ancestors revel in such news? Their progeny [descendant] had been asked to participate at the highest level . . . in the highest place in our country. . . . I was bowled over! I was flabbergasted! I was delighted.[1]

Getting to Work

Angelou knew she did not have time to spare. The inauguration was weeks away, and she needed to get busy. She approached this project as she did all her writing projects. Instead of working in her spacious redbrick North Carolina home, she checked into a nearby hotel. She had learned long ago how difficult it could be to work at home—there were too many things she loved there, too many things that could distract her from writing.

President Bill Clinton asked Angelou to write a poem and read it during his 1993 inauguration. Angelou was "flabbergasted" and "delighted."

She took a few things with her to the hotel—a Bible, a yellow notepad, and a deck of cards. She had found over the years that playing solitaire gave her hands something to do while she was thinking. When she needed a break, she would walk outside. But there were distractions there, too. It seemed that everyone knew she was working on the inaugural poem.

"People stop me on the street and in hotel lobbies and say, 'Please say something,'" Angelou told one reporter. "Whites ask, 'Will you please say something to stop the hate?' Black people say, 'Tell our story.'"[2]

As the inauguration date drew closer, she began feeling afraid. It was already such a great responsibility. But it seemed to be growing. She needed to write a poem that spoke not only to individual Americans, but also to Americans as a people. And it had to be a poem that could resonate with all of her listeners. "I'm terrified, terrified,"[3] she admitted, just days before the poem had to be finished.

Finding Her Voice

To anyone who knew Maya Angelou, or who had read her books, such fear seemed uncharacteristic. She had written twelve books, including six volumes of poetry. She had traveled all over the world and had worked as a singer, a dancer, and a teacher. She had fought for civil rights with Martin Luther King Jr. and Malcolm X.

Angelou was a person who had faced great challenges in her personal life, too. She survived

Angelou recites her poem "On the Pulse of the Morning" during the 1993 inauguration of President Bill Clinton.

rape when she was seven years old. She was a single mother at sixteen. She had grown up in the South when racial segregation was a fact of life. Yet she had managed to become stronger with each battle, finding the voice within her that gave her confidence.

By January 23, 1993, Maya Angelou found her voice once more. At the inauguration she walked to the podium and looked out at the sea of people before her. More than 250,000 people were there, many of them waving small American flags. Hundreds of millions more—in the United States and around the world—were watching on television. This was the time for her words to be heard. Maya Angelou took a deep breath, looked at the poem before her, and began to speak.

Chapter 1

A Childhood in Stamps

Maya Angelou was born Marguerite Ann Johnson in St. Louis, Missouri, on April 4, 1928. Her father, Bailey Johnson, worked as a doorman at a hotel in St. Louis, and her mother, Vivian Baxter Johnson, was a card dealer in an illegal gambling parlor. Angelou had a brother, Bailey Jr., who was a year older than she.

It was her brother who gave her the name by which she would always be known. When the two were very little, Bailey had trouble saying "Marguerite." Instead, he called her "My Sister." Eventually, that got shortened to "My" and then became "Maya."

"To Whom It May Concern"

When Angelou was three, her parents divorced. At the time, the family was living in Long Beach, California. Because their marriage was falling apart, the Johnsons sent Maya and Bailey to live with their father's mother in Stamps, Arkansas. They thought it best for the children to live in a more stable environment. The two children were put on a train in California for the long journey, traveling all alone.

It seems almost unimaginable in the twenty-first century that a three-year-old and a four-year-old would be made to travel across the country by themselves. But in those days, young children were sometimes sent to relatives during times of family crisis. In her autobiography, *I Know Why the Caged Bird Sings*, Angelou says that one of her first memories is of her and Bailey sitting on the train, with tags around their wrists. The tags contained a "To Whom It May Concern" note explaining that they were Marguerite and Bailey Johnson Jr. from Long Beach, California, on their way to Stamps, Arkansas, to meet Mrs. Annie Henderson.

Mrs. Annie Henderson was their grandmother, whom Maya and Bailey called Momma. At 6 feet 2 inches (1.9m), she was the tallest woman Maya had ever seen. Momma and her son, the children's Uncle Willie, would be Maya and Bailey's only family for most of their childhood.

The Store

Life in the little town of Stamps, Arkansas, was far different from what the children had known in California. Their home was the rear of the William Johnson General Merchandise Store, which Momma owned. Maya shared a bed with Momma, while Bailey slept with Uncle Willie. There was an outhouse out back, and no running water or electricity. Everyone—even young children like Maya and Bailey—had jobs to do.

"The Store," as it was known to the residents of Stamps, was located in the African American section of the town known as the Quarters. It was a place to buy groceries and other goods. Momma's meat pies were fresh each day, and many customers came in for lunch. On nice days, the local barber would give haircuts on the front porch. Finally, it was a place for people from the Quarters to gather—to talk, laugh, and exchange news and gossip.

For little Maya, the Store was her favorite place in the world:

It was a glorious place. I remember the wonderful smells; the aroma of the pickle barrel, the bulging sacks of corn, the luscious ripe fruit. You could pick up a can of snuff from North Carolina, a box of matches from Ohio, a yard of ribbon from New York. All of those places seemed terribly exotic to me. I would fantasize how people from there had actually touched those objects. It was a magnificent experience![4]

As a child, Maya spent her days at "The Store," the business her grandmother owned. The general store, similar to the one pictured here, was like a meeting place for African Americans in the South.

A Strong Role Model

Momma and Uncle Willie were both strong personalities, and they took their responsibility of raising two young children seriously. Momma was a firm believer in not buying anything that she could make herself, so she sewed all of their clothes. Angelou later recalled that she and Bailey "looked like walking wallpaper—all our clothes were made out of the same material."[5]

When the children began attending school, Uncle Willie over-saw their homework. Willie, who was severely crippled from a child-hood accident, sat with them each day as they did their work. He did not tolerate sloppiness or carelessness, and it was not until the homework was done—and done well—that Maya and Bailey could go out to play with the other children in the neighborhood.

Church was a big part of Maya and Bailey's life in Stamps. Rather than just a Sunday commitment, as Angelou explained years later to journalist Bill Moyers, being part of the Christian Methodist Episcopal Church in Stamps was an all-week affair:

> We went to church all day Sunday. Then on Monday evening we went to missionary meetings. Tuesday evening, usher boy meetings. Wednesday, prayer meeting. Thurs-day evening, choir practice. We went to church all the time, and at all those meetings, we sang.[6]

Angelou insists that her experiences singing in church as a child were a huge influence on her poetry later on. "Actually," she says, "the first poetry I ever knew was the poetry of the gospel songs and the spirituals. I knew that blacks had written the music. I thought it was marvelous stuff!"[7]

Separate but Not Equal

These early years in Stamps were largely happy ones. But as loved as Maya felt by Momma and Uncle Willie, she was learning that there was an ugliness about the town, too. Like the rest of the South in the 1930s, racial inequality was normal. Although slav-ery had been abolished since President Abraham Lincoln signed the Emancipation Proclamation in 1863, little had changed for African Americans in the following seventy-some years.

As Maya was learning, society in the South was controlled by whites. Laws forbade blacks from being seated at restaurants. They could not use the same drinking fountains or bathrooms as whites. Other laws made it very difficult for blacks to own property.

Maya was aware that the town of Stamps was divided. The Quarters was black, and was separated from the white part of town by railroad tracks and the Red River. Most black residents

Racial inequality was common in the South in the 1930s. There were separate drinking fountains and bathrooms for blacks and whites, and blacks were forbidden from being seated at restaurants.

of Stamps worked for white plantation owners. They picked cotton or worked as maids in white homes.

"We Covered Him with Potatoes and Onions"

The racial inequality that kept black people poor was an unfortunate part of everyday life in the South. But in Stamps, Maya learned something that was even more frightening and upsetting. It was that the black residents could be hated—and even killed—for no reason at all.

The Ku Klux Klan was active in Stamps. The Klan was a white terrorist organization that beat, tortured, and lynched blacks. Its members burned crosses on the lawns of whites who sympathized with black residents. One afternoon Maya and Bailey saw firsthand how worried people in the Quarters were when the Klan was rumored to be assembling for one of their nighttime raids.

A black man was alleged to have spoken rudely to a white woman in Stamps. For that reason, the Klan was going to strike that night and search for that man. The sheriff of Stamps, who

The Ku Klux Klan was active in Stamps. One night, Momma, Maya, and Bailey had to hide Uncle Willie because the Klan was rumored to have been planning a nighttime raid in the town.

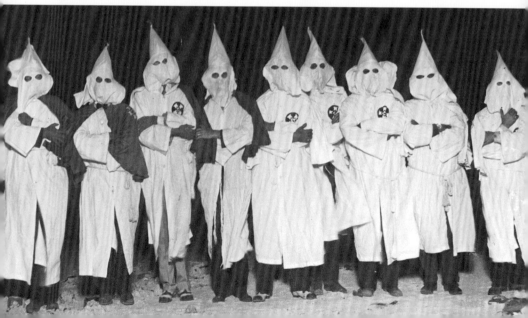

had no control over the organization, came to the Store to warn Momma and Uncle Willie. Every black man was in danger.

Momma quickly got busy hiding Willie. She enlisted the help of Maya and Bailey, too:

> We were told to take the potatoes and onions out of their bins and knock out the dividing walls that kept them apart. Then with a tedious and fearful slowness Uncle Willie gave me his rubber tipped cane and bent down to get into the now-enlarged empty bin. It took forever before he lay down flat, and then we covered him with potatoes and onions, layer upon layer, like a casserole.[8]

A Sad Lesson

As time went on, Maya learned that in the South, even young children could be personally affected by racial hatred. In a 1997 interview, she recalled a time that Momma allowed her and Bailey to go to the movie theater when she was very young. Angelou remembers what happened when she went up to the white girl who was taking tickets and asked to buy one:

> The girl took my dime, and she wouldn't put her hand on it. I put it down. She had a cigar box, and she took a card and raked my dime into the cigar box. Now the white kids got tickets. She took their money, and she gave them little stubs. She didn't give us anything. She just motioned, which meant that we had to go up the side steps, outside steps, and crawl through a really crummy little door, and sit perched on these three or four benches to watch the movie. And all because I was black. And I thought, "Well, I don't think I'll be going to the movies a lot.[9]

"The Greatest Person in My World"

No matter what life threw at her in Stamps, Maya could always count on Bailey for support. While she was shy and withdrawn, Bailey was a natural leader, with a quick wit. Maya was self-conscious about her appearance—especially her light complexion and hair that resembled "black steel wool." Bailey was quite the opposite. He had long black curls, and he was praised "for his velvet-black skin."[10]

It was Bailey who could silently steal pickles out of the barrel that sat close to Uncle Willie in the Store—and share them with Maya. It was Bailey with whom she shared a secret language (pig latin) with which they could communicate without adults knowing what they were saying.

In her book, *I Know Why the Caged Bird Sings*, Angelou stresses how deeply she loved her brother:

> Bailey was the greatest person in my world. And the fact that he was my brother, my only brother, and I had no sisters to share him with, was such good fortune that it made me want to live a Christian life just to show God that I was grateful.[11]

Gifts

Life went on as the children became secure and happy in their new home. However, one Christmas, about three years after they came to Stamps, Maya and Bailey received an interesting package in the mail. It turned out to contain Christmas presents from their parents, who were living separately in California. Interestingly, instead of being excited by these gifts, Maya and Bailey were shattered.

They had been very little when their parents put them on that train three years before. Maya, the younger of the two, barely remembered her mother and father. Both of the children had been too little to understand divorce. Instead, Maya had constructed a fantasy that her parents were really dead. In her mind, having dead parents was more comforting than having living parents who had abandoned her and Bailey.

For some reason, that Christmas their father and mother had sent them presents. Maya's gift from her mother was a tea set and a blonde, blue-eyed doll. Their father had sent the children a photograph of himself. Instead of being happy, Maya and Bailey both cried when they opened their gifts. Later she would recall that their tears were a reaction to the difficult questions that those gifts brought up. For example, if their parents were not dead and were able to send gifts, then why had they not heard from them in three

Momma's Store

In *I Know Why the Caged Bird Sings*, Angelou describes the Store, where she and Bailey spent most of their time while living in Stamps. It is clear from her descriptions, that the place never looked exactly the same at different hours of the day. Angelou writes:

> Alone and empty in the mornings, it looked like an un-opened present from a stranger. Opening the front doors was pulling the ribbon off the unexpected gift. The light would come in softly (we faced north), easing itself over the shelves of mackerel, salmon, tobacco, thread. It fell flat on the big vat of lard and by noon-time during the summer, the grease had softened to a thick soup.

> Whenever I walked into the Store in the afternoon, I sensed that it was tired. I alone could hear the slow pulse of its job half done. But just before bedtime, after numerous people had walked in and out, had argued over their bills, or joked about their neighbors, or just dropped in to give Sister Henderson a "Hi, y'all," the promise of magic mornings returned to the store and spread itself over the family in washed life waves.

Maya Angelou, *The Collected Autobiographies of Maya Angelou*. New York: Modern Library, 2004, p. 17.

years? Why had they been sent away in the first place? As Maya wondered, "What did we do so wrong? . . . Why, at three and four, did we have tags put on our arms to be sent by train alone from Long Beach, California to Stamps, Arkansas?"[12]

The Return of Daddy Bailey

The Christmas gifts had been upsetting, but the sudden appearance of their father a year later turned the children's world upside down. Daddy Bailey, as he was called, was extraordinarily handsome. He was loud, he laughed a lot, and after three weeks of staying at the Store with them all, he stunned Maya and Bailey by announcing that he was leaving—and taking them with him.

Bailey was excited, but seven-year-old Maya was very upset. She was unsure about her father and was frightened to leave Stamps and Momma. She did not want to be separated from Bailey, however. She loved him dearly—he was often her only ally. So she resigned herself to leaving, and watched as Momma sewed new jumpers and skirts for her new life.

Soon, she and Bailey were sitting in Daddy Bailey's gray De-Soto. Bailey was having the time of his life. Clearly, he had decided that having a father was very exciting. But Maya sat in the back, sad and unsure of what her life was going to be like. She assumed she and Bailey were going to California with their father. But she and Bailey were both shocked when Daddy Bailey told them he was taking them to St. Louis, so they could live with their mother.

Maya was both nervous about leaving Stamps and worried about how her mother would treat her. She and Bailey had talked a lot about feeling rejected by their parents. Added to that, Maya had become very self-conscious about how she looked. She had been teased by some children in Stamps for being so light skinned. She often had compared herself with other girls and believed that she came up short. She fantasized about having long blonde hair and blue eyes. She described herself as "a too-big Negro girl, with nappy [tightly curled] black hair, broad feet and a space between her teeth that would hold a number two pencil."[13] If her mother was beautiful and was dissatisfied with her daughter's looks, Maya believed, life would be very difficult.

Meeting Mother Dear

Maya had been born in St. Louis, but she found nothing at all familiar about the city. "St. Louis was a new kind of hot and a new kind of dirty," she later wrote. "My memories had no pictures of the crowded-together soot-covered buildings. For all I knew, we were being driven to hell and our father was the delivering devil."[14]

But while Maya had been nervous about meeting her mother, worrying that she would be rejected again, she need not have been anxious at all. Their mother was excited to see her children, and they were amazed at how beautiful she was. Bailey fell head over heels in love with her and began calling her "Mother Dear." Maya, on the other hand, felt that she understood why her mother had abandoned her. "She was too beautiful to have children," she wrote. "I had never seen a woman as pretty as she who was called 'Mother.'"[15]

Maya and Bailey stayed with their mother at Grandfather Baxter's home. It was a big house on Carolina Street in the African American section of St. Louis. Mother was not around much. She worked long hours and late nights as a card dealer in gambling parlors. Grandmother kept track of the two children while Mother was at work.

The fountain at Union Square in St. Louis. When Maya was seven years old, she and her brother returned to the town in which they were born to live with their mother.

Not an Easy Transition

Although there was plenty of room in the Baxter house, it was very difficult for the children to get used to the city. The factories made the air dirty and smelly. The noise from buses, trains, and even toilets flushing (there was only an outhouse at Momma's) seemed never ending.

Even the food was different. For the first time, the children had thin-sliced ham—a huge change from the thick slabs they ate for breakfast back in Stamps. In fact, for a while, Maya was sure that the thin-sliced meat was a delicacy. She and Bailey were also introduced to a mixture of jelly beans and peanuts. In Stamps, peanuts were brought in raw from the fields and roasted. They had never been served with jelly beans.

The school in St. Louis was quite a change from their school in Stamps, too. Uncle Willie had overseen their homework each day, and as a result, Bailey and Maya were ahead of their class in this new school. The two felt that the students at this new school seemed far behind in their work. The teachers were different, too. They seemed arrogant, as though they were talking down to the students. Although she did not enjoy school, Maya was excited to get her first library card and spent almost every Saturday reading and checking out books from the public library.

Mr. Freeman

About six months after they arrived in St. Louis, Mother moved Maya and Bailey into a house she shared with her boyfriend, Mr. Freeman. He worked at the railroad yards and usually did not come home until later in the evening, after the children had eaten dinner. Most of the time Freeman paid little attention to the children.

One morning, however, Bailey left to play baseball with friends, and just as Maya was about to leave for the library, Freeman raped her. Afterward, he threatened that if she told Bailey what happened, he would kill him. Then Freeman told her to go to the library. Terrified at his threat of killing her brother and injured from the rape, Maya did as she was told. Walking to the library, however, she felt as though her hips were coming out of their sockets. Once she arrived, sitting on the hard library chairs made the pain even worse. She went home, hid her stained underwear under her mattress, and crawled under the covers. She believed that the pain was God's punishment—that somehow what had happened was her fault.

Getting Liver

In *Hallelujah! The Welcome Table,* Angelou recalls that twice a year, Momma would decide that they needed to eat liver—fresh meat that was available only by going to the butcher on the white side of Stamps. She and Bailey were the ones sent to buy it, a journey that was both fun and frightening. Angelou writes:

> Crossing our area of Stamps, which in childhood's narrow measure seemed a whole world, obliged us by custom to stop and speak to every black person we met. Bailey also felt constrained to spend a few minutes playing with each friend. There I felt a special joy in going through the black area with time on our hands and money in our pockets. . . . But the pleasure fled when we reached the white part of town. Suddenly we were explorers walking without weapons into man-eating animals' territory.

> We never turned to look at the houses we passed, nor did we really speak to each other once we were in enemy territory. We solemnly moved forward to our goal. At the butcher shop we were lucky if no one came in. All whites were served before us, even if the butcher was half into our order. In fact, a black maid or cook would be served before us, because her order was intended for white people. . . .

> We would get the liver Momma wanted . . . and make our way back across the white zone.

Maya Angelou, *Hallelujah! The Welcome Table: A Lifetime of Memories with Recipes.* New York: Random House, 2004, p. 46.

Her mother found the stained underwear the next day as she changed the sheets on the bed. She rushed Maya to the hospital, and Bailey was devastated. He insisted that she tell him who had raped her. Although she refused at first, she finally told him that it was Mr. Freeman. Bailey told Grandmother Baxter, who called the police. Freeman was arrested immediately.

Worse and Worse

As painful as the rape had been for Maya, the trial and its aftermath were far worse. Even though she was only seven-and-a-half years old, she had to take the stand and testify against Freeman. Freeman was found guilty and sentenced to a year and one day. However, for a reason that was not explained, his lawyer got him released from custody before he had served his sentence.

The next evening, Maya and Bailey were visitng at the Baxter house playing Monopoly. A policeman came to the door and told Grandmother Baxter that Freeman had been found dead in the lot behind the slaughterhouse. According to the policeman, Freeman had been kicked to death.

Maya believed that Freeman's death—however it happened—was her fault. She had told the lawyers and the judge what Freeman had done. And afterward, he had been killed. In her seven-year-old mind, it made perfect sense. Her voice had killed a man. And she decided that day that she would not speak again. If she did speak, she believed, another person would surely die:

> I could feel the evilness flowing through my body and waiting, pent up, to rush off my tongue if I tried to open my mouth. I clamped my teeth shut, I'd hold it in. If it escaped, wouldn't it flood the whole world and all the innocent people?[16]

Silence and Tears

Soon Maya and Bailey moved back into the Baxters' house. Grandmother Baxter tried hard to make Maya feel better. Mother tried, too. Bailey was the one person she would talk to, but only because she loved him so much and she was sure that her love would protect him. To talk to other people was far too risky, she believed. So the days became months. Still, she was mute.

At first everyone tried to be patient. But the little girl's silence was perplexing to her family. They finally decided she and Bailey might do better back in Stamps. Although Bailey remained loyal to Maya, he cried as they left St. Louis. He had grown to love his Mother and was heartbroken that he was leaving her behind.

Chapter 2

Turning Points

Maya continued her silence in Stamps. She spoke rarely, only when absolutely necessary. Many people in Stamps just assumed she was sensitive, or maybe that she missed her family in St. Louis. Quite a few thought she might be developmentally delayed. But no one got angry with her, as they had in St. Louis.

Momma was patient. She told Maya that when she was ready, she would speak. Years later, Angelou remembered Momma's words of encouragement—telling her that when she began to speak, God would make sure she had great things to say:

> Sister, Momma don't care what these people say: "You must be an idiot, you must be a moron." Momma don't care, sister. Momma know, when you and the Good Lord get ready, you're gonna be a preacher." Well, I used to sit and think to myself, "Poor, ignorant Momma. She doesn't know. I will never speak, let alone preach."[17]

A Good Listener

But while Maya did not speak, she was not moping either. She did her chores, and when she had time to herself, she remained busy. She developed a skill that would later help her become a writer—listening. She became good at absorbing the talk that was everywhere around her. She became attuned to the lilt and rhythms of voices.

She continued reading as an escape. She grew to love the novels of Charlotte Brontë, such as *Jane Eyre*, as well as the poems and stories of Edgar Allan Poe. Even though she was a poor black girl in the American South, the troubles of other people in other places around the world resonated with her. Everyone had problems, and it was comforting to read about how other people dealt with theirs.

But the most stirring of the writers she encountered was William Shakespeare. She was fascinated by how rhythmic and musical Shakespeare's writing was—especially his sonnets. In a 1981 interview with journalist Bill Moyers, she recalled reading Sonnet 29, which begins, "When in disgrace with fortune and men's eyes/I all alone beweep my outcast state."

William Shakespeare was Angelou's favorite writer growing up. His sonnets were fascinating to the young girl, who described them as "rhythmic and musical."

"I wept," she told Moyers, "because I thought myself *certainly* in disgrace with fortune—being black and poor and female in the South, and I was also out of grace with men's eyes, because I wasn't pretty."[18]

Mrs. Flowers

But as the weeks and months of silence turned into years, Momma decided that something needed to be done. Maya was ten years old, and spoke no more than she had three years before. Although Maya did not realize it at the time, Momma asked a friend, Bertha Flowers, for help.

Flowers was the wealthiest black woman in Stamps. She was also beautiful and obviously well educated. Maya had frequently marveled that Momma and Flowers could be friends. In fact, she would sometimes wince when she overheard Momma use incorrect grammar when speaking to Mrs. Flowers. But although it seemed unlikely to Maya, the two were indeed friends. "Mrs. Flowers was highly educated and my grandmother wasn't," recalled Angelou later. "But they were a pair, like coffee and cake."[19]

Not long afterwards, Mrs. Flowers came to the store and asked Maya to carry her packages home. As they walked, Flowers began talking to Maya, apparently not concerned that the girl did not speak back. When they got to the house, she served Maya iced lemonade and buttery tea cookies, and began to tell her about books. She picked up a copy of Charles Dickens's *A Tale of Two Cities*, and began to read: "It was the best of times, it was the worst of times."[20]

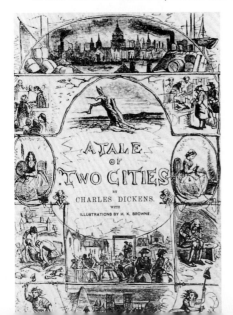

Because Maya would not start talking again, family friend Mrs. Flowers became her mentor. Mrs. Flowers read Charles Dickens's A Tale of Two Cities *to Maya, who soon thereafter began to speak again.*

Angelou said later that while she had read the book before, she had never experienced it like that. Listening to Flowers read those words, hearing them out loud, gave the story a whole new meaning. "She told me over and over," recalls Angelou, "that poetry was music written for the human voice."[21] Mrs. Flowers explained to Maya that words have more meaning that what is set down on the paper—that it takes a voice to bring out the deeper meanings in them.

A Lifeline

From that day on, Mrs. Flowers took Maya under her wing. She urged Maya to visit her on a regular basis. She was to bring poems that she read, too. Most importantly, she wanted Maya to practice reading them aloud and to listen to how her own voice made the poems that much more meaningful.

Maya did as she was asked. She found a little private space, under Momma's high bed. She could go underneath and read and practice saying the poems aloud. When she felt she was ready, she would go to Mrs. Flowers's home and recite them.

The attention that Mrs. Flowers gave her, and the education she shared, was a turning point in Maya's life. Not only did she become more comfortable with her own voice, but she also became more confident around other people. After all, if the most elegant black lady in Stamps found her likeable, other people surely would. And it was Mrs. Flowers, she insists, who made all the difference. She was "the lady who threw me my first lifeline . . . one of the few gentlewomen I have ever known and has remained throughout my life the full measure of what a human being can be."[22]

Star Pupil

Of course, Maya's healing from the rape did not happen overnight. But little by little, she began to be braver, a bit more outgoing. She made her very first friend, a girl named Louise Kendricks. "I was liked," she wrote later, "and what a difference it made. I was respected not as Mrs. Henderson's grandchild or Bailey's sister, but just for being Marguerite Johnson."[23]

She also became even more absorbed by books than she had been before. And before long, she began writing her own poetry. She looked forward to graduation from eighth grade. She was one of the top students in her class, and the ceremony was going to be a high point for her.

The day of graduation was like a dream for Maya. She had a brand-new dress she was excited to wear. That morning, Momma and Uncle Willie presented her with a Mickey Mouse watch. Bailey gave her a leather-bound collection of poems by Edgar Allan Poe. She was so happy she turned to one of her favorite poems, "Annabel Lee," and the two of them walked up and down the

A Long Legacy of Poetry

In her book of essays, *Even the Stars Look Lonesome*, Angelou talks about how long poetry as been part of African Americans' lives, and how important it has always been. She writes:

> In that little town in Arkansas, whenever my grandmother saw me reading poetry, she would say, "Sister, Momma loves to see you read the poetry because that will put starch in your backbone." When people who were enslaved, whose wrists were bound and whose ankles were tied, sang,

> I'm gonna run on,
> See what the end is gonna be. . . .
> I'm gonna run on,
> See what the end is gonna be. . . .

> the singer and the audience were made to understand that, however we had arrived here, under whatever bludgeoning of chance, we were the stuff out of which nations and dreams were made and that we had come here to stay.

Maya Angelou, *Even the Stars Look Lonesome.* New York: Random House, 1997, pp. 130–31.

rows of the garden, "the cool dirt between our toes, reciting the beautifully sad lines."[24] Even the customers at the store were generous, pressing nickels and dimes into her hands and offering congratulations to her. For Maya, now twelve, there had never been a more beautiful day.

An Ugly Speech

The ceremony was similar to most graduations at that time. A minister came and led them in prayer. Everyone sang "The Star-Spangled Banner." The principal said a few words. And then the guest speaker, a white politician from Texarkana, Arkansas, began to talk.

The politician talked about white schools in Arkansas and how graduates from those places would have many opportunities in life. Some might go on to be artists, inventors, or scientists. He emphasized that blacks and whites were not equal, and that of course, black opportunities were different. His words were terribly depressing to the graduates, who, moments before, had been excited and full of hope. Here was another reminder that even on their graduation day, they could only look forward to careers as maids, handymen, and—if they were very lucky—athletes.

For Maya and her classmates, the magic had gone out of the day, until Henry Reed stood up. He was the class's smartest member and had been chosen to give a special speech. After delivering the speech, Henry did something totally unexpected. He turned to face his classmates and started to sing. It was a beautiful song called "Lift Ev'ry Voice and Sing," which was referred to by some African Americans as "the black national anthem."

Everyone—even the youngest child—knew it by heart. They had sung it thousands of times in church. But as everyone joined in to sing it, for Maya the song became very personal. The hope it proclaimed had to do with her own hope and that of her classmates who were beginning their new lives. After the song was over, she remembers, "I was no longer simply a member of the proud graduating class of 1940: I was a proud member of the wonderful, beautiful Negro race."[25]

A Good Time to Leave

Not long after graduation, Momma announced that it was time for Maya and Bailey to leave Stamps. It would always be their home, she insisted, but it was a good time to find more opportunities. And there were certainly be more of those in California, where both of their parents now lived, than in Stamps.

Although Momma never said so, Maya and Bailey believed that the real reason she wanted them to leave Stamps was because of an incident that had happened a few weeks before. Bailey had run home terrified and sickened. He had seen the bloated body of a black man pulled out of the river. The man's genitals had been cut off, and the white policemen were standing around and joking. Bailey, frightened by what he had seen, wanted to know why whites hated black people so much. Neither Momma nor Uncle Willie could help Bailey, for the question really had no answer.

Soon after that incident, the travel plans were made. They would go by train—Momma and Maya first, and then, when there was enough money, Bailey would join them. Momma would stay with the children in Los Angeles near their father until Mother Dear could get a place large enough for them in San Francisco, where she currently lived.

Back with Mother Dear

Six months later they were established in San Francisco, and Momma returned to Arkansas. Maya and Bailey began a new kind of life in a house with Mother, Grandmother Baxter, and two of their uncles. And while there had been many rules and responsibilities in Momma's house in Stamps, life with Mother was more spontaneous and carefree. She sometimes woke them up in the middle of the night to talk, laugh, and watch her dance the Time Step or the Suzy Q. She loved making them hot chocolate and biscuits—no matter what the time of day or night.

Mother also helped them learn more about city life. She showed them the gambling parlor where she sometimes played cards for money and the one where she ran a poker game. She enjoyed herself and enjoyed having her children around. And more and more, Maya grew to love the city.

She also realized that racism, which was very evident back in Stamps, existed in San Francisco, too. Several months before, in December 1941, the Japanese had bombed Pearl Harbor. San Francisco was a large shipbuilding center and housed a huge naval base. Maya noted how Japanese Americans were looked at with distrust, no matter how long they had lived in the United States. It was during this time that the government insisted that any people of Japanese descent must abandon their homes and businesses and move to detention camps. Government officials worried that Japanese

Maya saw a different kind of racism in San Francisco when she was living with her mother. After the bombing of Pearl Harbor, she noticed that Japanese Americans were looked at with distrust, and they were sent away to relocation camps.

Americans might communicate with Japanese troops, aiding them in their fight against America. Maya noticed their absence, as families were rounded up and taken to detention camps—disappearing from the city "soundlessly and without protest."[26]

A New School

Maya attended an all-girls high school near her home. But it was difficult for her to settle in. There was a great deal of unrest among the students—from the Mexican girls who hid knives in their tall hairdos, to the African American girls who fought constantly. Maya was relieved when she was able to transfer to George Washington High School. Although she was one of only three black students, this school did not have the same racial strife as the other did.

One thing Maya learned quickly was that although she had been a top student in her other schools, she had to work much harder at George Washington. These students were far better prepared than those at her other schools. Since being a top student had long been a big part of her identity, Maya started feeling unsure of herself, doubting whether she had the ability to do well.

Luckily, she had a teacher who helped rebuild her self-esteem. Miss Kirwin taught civics and current events. Unlike Mrs. Flowers back in Stamps, Miss Kirwin did not single Maya out or give her special attention. Instead, she treated all her students as her equals, with respect and dignity. She taught, not with textbooks, but with *Time* magazine and the daily newspapers. Maya excitedly began taking an interest in world events and living up to the high expectations Miss Kirwin had for her and her classmates.

In addition to her classes during the day, Maya unexpectedly—and mysteriously— received a scholarship to the California Labor School. Actually an adult college, the Labor School offered evening classes for younger students. Maya signed up for drama. Bailey and Mother talked her into registering for a dance class, too.

Visiting Daddy Bailey

In the summer of 1943, fifteen-year-old Maya got an invitation from her father to spend time with him down in Los Angeles.

Daddy had a girlfriend named Dolores, who told Maya that she would meet her at the train station. When Maya arrived, she was shocked to see that Dolores was only a few years older than she. Dolores was equally shocked—Bailey Sr. had told her that Maya was eight years old.

The difficult meeting between the two was only the beginning of their strained relationship. Dolores clearly disliked her, and one night she insulted Maya's mother. Shocked, Maya slapped Dolores. The two struggled, and Maya broke free. She ran to her father's car and locked herself inside, while Dolores circled the car, screaming, a hammer in her hand. It did not take long for Maya to realize she was bleeding—during their struggle, Dolores had stabbed her.

When Daddy Bailey intervened, he realized Maya was hurt. He also realized that taking her to the hospital would create a scandal. Instead, he took her to the home of a friend, who treated her cut with witch hazel and Band-Aids. Although he promised he would come back to see her that evening, he left her there.

Homeless in Los Angeles

Maya was determined not to return to her father's house. She did not want to have any further contact with Dolores, who no doubt felt the same way about her. She hastily raided the cupboards while the owners of the house were at work, made herself several tuna salad sandwiches, grabbed a handful of bandages, and left.

Unsure of what to do, Maya went to the library and read for awhile. She had passed a junkyard filled with old cars, and as evening came, decided that she could sleep in one of them that evening. The next morning, she awoke to the sight of curious faces staring at her through the car's windows.

They were homeless teenagers—black, white, and Mexican. They, too, slept in the junkyard, and had created a loose-knit family. They all worked at odd jobs during the day and pooled their money. Their leader, a boy named Bootsie, told Maya that she could stay, but there were rules. Sleeping with members of the opposite sex was forbidden, as was stealing. Everybody worked, too—whether collecting bottles, mowing lawns, or running errands for some of the nearby shopkeepers. Maya agreed to the rules and spent the next six weeks with this community of teenagers in the junkyard.

Skipping a Semester

Maya finally called Mother in San Francisco and arranged to return home. She was excited to see Bailey and her mother again, but in her absence, things had changed. Bailey had become more independent, spending his time with a rough group of friends. His language had changed, too, Maya noticed. "He was forever dropping slangy terms into his sentences like dumplings in a pot."[27] He was also having a relationship with a white prostitute, which infuriated Mother. After she insisted that he follow her rules or move out, Bailey refused and left home.

Maya understood Mother's frustration with Bailey. However, without her brother, the house was very dull—having "all the cheeriness of a dungeon and the appeal of a tomb."[28] Maya decided that she needed to do something other than live there and continue to go to school. She talked her mother into allowing her to take a semester off. She could get a job for awhile and go back to school later.

At fifteen, her dream job was being a conductor on the San Francisco trolley system. The blue uniform was appealing, as was the idea of a money changer around her waist. But the trolley company had never had a black conductor. For weeks, she went to the office, asking to meet with someone about the job. Although she was turned away several times by the receptionist, she finally was allowed to fill out an application. She lied about her age (saying she was nineteen) and got the job.

A Question and a Baby

When the next semester of school began, Maya did not feel ready to return. Between the six weeks of living with the homeless teenagers in Los Angeles and her new job, school did not have the allure it once had. Maya began to cut classes and just walk around the city. During this time, she began to feel as though she

Maya returned once again to San Francisco to live with her mother. At age fifteen, she took a semester off of school and got a job as a trolley conductor.

wanted a boyfriend. For years she had felt unfeminine—too tall, too skinny, and with feet too big. She wondered if down deep she was a boy. Having a boyfriend would answer such questions, she decided. She chose one of the best-looking boys in the neighborhood and asked if he would have sex with her.

The boy agreed, and afterward, they went their separate ways. Maya did not have long to think about whether her question about her gender had been answered. In three weeks' time, she learned that she was pregnant. "The world had ended," she wrote later, "and I was the only person who knew it."[29] She felt angry with herself, and fearful of what lay ahead.

She wrote to Bailey, who was at sea with the merchant marine. He advised her not to tell Mother, for she would order Maya to quit school. Bailey reminded her that if she were to quit before graduating, it would be very hard to go back later. Amazingly, Maya was able to keep the pregnancy a secret from Mother and her new stepfather, Daddy Clidell Jackson. She wore baggy cloth-

Annie Henderson's Idea

It was a rarity for any African American to own property back in Annie Henderson's day, but even more rare for a woman. In 1903 her husband abandoned her, leaving her with their two young children and no job. She decided to do what she did best, which was cook. She devised a plan to sell her homemade meat pies outside each of Stamps's biggest employers, the cotton gin and the lumber mill. She began frying the pies just a half hour before the lunch bell rang. Hungry workers flocked to her stand and bought the chicken and ham pies for five cents each. She visited each site every other day.

Eventually, she built a little hut between the cotton mill and the lumberyard, so she could double her lunchtime business. That hut eventually became the Store. It remained the hub of the black community in Stamps for more than sixty years.

ing that hid her growing belly. Fighting morning sickness and feeling guilty about keeping such a secret from her mother, Maya was able to accomplish her goal. In May 1945 she graduated from high school without anyone having found out her secret.

Clyde

The night of graduation, Maya knew she had to tell her mother and stepfather. Too nervous to tell them outright, she left a note on their bed. In the note she apologized for bringing disgrace and shame on the family. Her parents were reasonable, but they had questions. Did Maya want to marry the boy? Did he want to marry her? The answer to both was "no."

Three weeks later, after a short labor, Maya gave birth to a son—Clyde Bailey Johnson. And while she was excited and proud of her new baby, it did not take long for her to realize that things would never be the same again.

Chapter 3

Out on Her Own

Now that Angelou had a baby, getting a job was more important than ever. Mother and Daddy Clidell suggested that she go on to college. They would be willing to take care of Clyde while she was at school. The idea of attending college was an enticing one for her.

But as much as Angelou had dreamed of attending college, she did not want to leave her new baby with her parents. For one thing, she could sense that their marriage was breaking down. Also, she could see that Mother was concerned about money. People were not spending money at the card parlors as they used to. The booming economy had ended with the war. Many people from the South who had come to San Francisco to work were returning home again—including those workers who had rented rooms in her parents' big house. Angelou did not want to be a financial burden to them.

But there was a deeper reason for not leaving Clyde and going to college—a reason that had festered since she was a little girl. She felt Mother had been very irresponsible with her and Bailey when they were little. She writes in her book, *Gather Together in My Name*, that her Mother "had left me with others until I was thirteen and why should she feel more responsibility for my child than she had felt for her own."[30] There was no way that Angelou would allow little Clyde to experience those same feelings that she had felt as a child.

Cooking Creole

She finally decided that the best thing for her and Clyde would be to get a job, and then, when she had enough money, they would move out of her parents' house. After being turned down for a job as a telephone operator, she walked by a restaurant with a Help Wanted sign in the window. The owner asked if she knew how to cook Creole, which is a mixture of African, Spanish, and French cooking. Not willing to give up the possibility of a job— especially one that paid $75 a week—she assured the woman that she was very good at Creole cooking. She was told she could start the following Monday.

Angelou knew that Papa Ford, an old man who still boarded at her parents' house, knew a lot about cooking. He assured her

With hopes of moving out of her parents' house with Clyde, Maya got a job cooking at a restaurant and learned to cook Creole.

that she could pretty much make any dish Creole by adding plenty of green peppers, onions, and garlic. Armed with this knowledge, she practiced her cooking all weekend and went to work on Monday with confidence.

Soon after she felt settled into her new job, she moved out of her parents' home and rented a room that had cooking privileges. With Mother's help, she found an elderly woman who would watch Clyde during the day. Angelou was excited and proud to be on her own, earning money and providing for her baby.

Curley

Angelou enjoyed working in the restaurant and in no time felt comfortable in her new role as cook and working mother. She met a customer named Curley, a navy man fourteen years older than she. Curley wanted to have a relationship with her, but explained that he was engaged. His fiancée lived in another state, and they would be getting married soon.

Young and naive, Angelou chose to ignore Curley's admission. She saw how good he was with her baby and enjoyed every minute she spent with him. When he finally left, as he had said he would, she was devastated. She had thought he would change his mind and stay. She wanted to be angry with Curley, but she realized she could not. "Because he had not lied, I was forbidden anger," she wrote later. "Because he had patiently and tenderly taught me love, I could not use hate to ease the pain. I had to bear it."[31]

Over the coming weeks, Angelou became more and more distraught. She was not eating or sleeping well. She finally sought out Bailey, who advised her that she needed a change of scene. He suggested that she take Clyde and leave San Francisco for a while. It was pointless to be depressed about Curley. She needed to get on with her life.

Mistakes

Angelou traveled south, to San Diego. After getting a job as a cocktail waitress at a nightclub called the Hi-Hat, she met Cleo and Henry Jenkins, a couple who offered her lodging as well as child care for Clyde. She busied herself working and earning money. She found a modern dance studio where she could take lessons. She also remembered how much she had enjoyed reading and began devouring books, as she once had done back in Stamps.

It was during this time, however, that Angelou entered into a scheme that she would come to regret. She had met two women prostitutes who were going to lose their house because they could not afford the payments. Maya had an idea: She could buy the house herself and take a percentage of the women's earnings. She began earning a lot more money, while not really working at it.

But one evening, she was struck by the danger of what she was doing. If the police discovered the business and found that she was the owner of the house, then she would be in huge trouble. Most frightening was the realization that she would be declared an unfit mother. Clyde would certainly be taken from her.

That night, she packed everything she owned, took Clyde, and sped to the train station, she recalled later, "as if the hounds of hell were coming to collect my soul."[32] She had done something incredibly risky and stupid. And now, she fled to the only place where she had ever felt truly safe.

Eight Days in Stamps

Angelou and Clyde arrived in Stamps, and Momma and Uncle Willie could not have been happier. They were both delighted to meet the baby, and at first it seemed that this trip was just what Angelou needed to regain her confidence.

But she had not been in the South for several years. Having lived in California, she was not used to the racial divisions that were the norm in Stamps. One day, she walked to the white section of Stamps to order a sewing pattern. In the store, she and the saleswoman were both in the same narrow aisle. Angelou was startled when the woman ordered her to wait, so that she—the saleswoman—could walk through first.

When she objected to being talked to in such a way, the saleswoman was startled. She was rude to Angelou, who countered with insults. Feeling that she had stuck up for herself, Angelou walked back to Momma's, only to be met with anger. Momma had received a call from the woman at the store. Insisting that it had been a matter of principle to speak up for herself, Angelou was stunned and hurt when Momma slapped her across the face, and told her how foolish her actions had been:

> You think 'cause you've been to California these crazy people won't kill you? . . . You think because of your all-fired principle some of the men won't feel like putting their white sheets on and riding over here to stir up trouble? You do, you're wrong. Ain't nothing to protect you and us except the Good Lord and some miles.[33]

Stung by Momma's anger, Angelou nonetheless followed her grandmother's orders and packed her and the baby's things and

The Split

Eager to show R.L. Poole that she was good enough to join his dance act, Angelou decided to do an impromptu routine for him which included doing the splits, as she recalls in *Gather Together in My Name*. She writes:

> I was unprepared for the movement (I had on a straight skirt), but R.L. was less ready than I. As my legs slipped apart and down, I lifted my arms in the graceful ballet position number 1 and I watched [his] face race from mild interest to incredulous. My hem caught mid-thigh and I felt my equilibrium teeter. With a quick sleight of hand I jerked up my skirt and continued my downward glide. . . . Unfortunately, I hadn't practiced the splits in months, so my pelvic bones resisted with force. I was only two inches from the floor, and I gave a couple of little bounces. . . . My skirt seams gave before my bones surrendered.

Maya Angelou, *The Collected Autobiographies of Maya Angelou*. New York: Modern Library, 2004, pp. 311–12.

left Stamps. She returned to San Francisco and her mother, still unsure about what she was going to do with herself.

Trying to Find a Place

The next months were difficult ones for Angelou. She tried to join the army, thinking that it would give her job training. It would also provide benefits once her service was through—including money for a home and college. She enlisted, gave away her civilian clothes, and quit her job while she waited to hear from the recruiters.

However, her army hopes died very soon. The administrators looked at her transcripts and saw that the California Labor School, where she had taken dance lessons in high school, had been declared a Communist organization. She would be a security risk, they told her, so she was forbidden from serving in the army.

Discouraged, Angelou took another job as a short-order cook. She spent lots of time in the neighborhood record store, where the owner introduced her to the newest jazz, calypso, gospel, and other types of music. She did not know what she wanted to do, but she was certain that working in a diner was only temporary. For now, she continued to drift and to dream about finding a place where she really fit in.

Poole and Rita

It was during this time that she met a man named R.L. Poole, a nightclub tap dancer who was looking for a new partner for his act. He had gotten her name from the owner of the record store, who knew Angelou had taken dance lessons as a girl. Although she had no experience in the kind of dancing Poole did, she threw herself into learning as much as she could, and Poole hired her.

They decided to call their act Poole and Rita (short for Marguerite). Dancing for a living opened up a whole new world for Angelou. Although Poole and Rita did not get a lot of jobs, she loved the excitement of performing in front of an audience. She felt as though she was learning more about dance, and she began to fall in love with Poole.

Not long after they had begun their act, however, Angelou was shocked when Poole's former partner showed up. She was ready to resume the act with Poole, and Angelou realized her career as a dancer was over, just as it had begun. Frustrated and discouraged, she felt as if she were going nowhere fast.

Rock Bottom

Deciding once again that a change of scenery would be best, Angelou and Clyde moved to Stockton, a town about 80 miles (129km) from the San Francisco Bay area. She took another job as a short-order cook and found Clyde a place to live during the week with a woman named Big Mary. On her days off, Angelou would pick up her son and spend the day with him. She continued to fantasize about meeting a man with whom she could build a life and who would be a good father for Clyde. She was using marijuana, too, to deal with the loneliness and frustration she felt.

After moving to Stockton with Clyde, Maya starting smoking marijuana to deal with the loneliness and frustration she felt over not having a man with whom to build a life or be a father to her son.

One night at the restaurant, she met a forty-five-year-old gambler named L.D. Tolbrook. He was married, but he told Angelou that he planned to leave his wife. Although Tolbrook was more than twice her age, they began a relationship. In Angelou's mind, he would eventually marry her and be a loving father to Clyde.

After racking up five thousand dollars in gambling debts, Tolbrook suggested that Angelou could help him pay off the men to whom he owed money. Eager to please him, she agreed, saying she would do anything to help. "Anything" turned out to be prostitution. Although she was not proud of what she was doing, she felt there was nothing wrong with her situation. "I reassured myself," she later wrote, "I was helping my man."[34]

Emergency

The plan was for her to spend a month as a prostitute, working every day. She saw Clyde for only a few hours at a time, and Big Mary was suspicious. She asked why Angelou could no longer take her son overnight. She questioned what kind of new job Angelou had.

Angelou had worries, too. She was spending so much time away from her son, her absence was affecting him. When she did see him, he clung to her as if he never wanted to let go. It made her feel guilty and ashamed. But she still believed that after a month, she would have made enough to help Tolbrook pay off his debts. In the long run, she thought, it would be worth it, and she and Clyde and Tolbrook would be a happy family.

One evening, she received a phone call from San Francisco. It was Papa Ford, one of her mother's roomers. He said that Mother was in the hospital and that Angelou needed to come home soon. After dropping the distraught Clyde off again at Big Mary's, she caught the first bus to San Francisco.

Losing Bailey

As it turned out, Mother's condition was not life threatening. But Eunice, Bailey's wife, was in the hospital at the same time with double pneumonia. Her condition deteriorated, and she died just before Angelou arrived—the day of her and Bailey's first anniversary.

Understandably, Bailey was grief stricken. But Angelou was even more concerned about her brother's apparent growing dependence on drugs, especially heroin. He had gone from being a happy person to being cynical and temperamental. A great deal of the change, she believed, was because of the group of young men that he hung around with. Even though he was physically right there with her, she felt as though she had completely lost her brother.

But even with his drug use, Bailey could see that his sister was in trouble, too. Angelou admitted to him that she was working temporarily as a prostitute for Tolbrook—just until he could pay off his gambling debts. But if she thought Bailey would be understanding, she was wrong. Bailey ordered her to get back to Stockton as quickly as she could, get the baby, and catch the next bus back home to San Francisco.

Losing Clyde

When she arrived at Big Mary's house, many days later than she had intended, Angelou was startled to find it boarded up and empty. As she stood there, panicking, a neighbor told her that Mary had moved three days ago. The other parents had come for their children, but she had not come for Clyde. And no one seemed to know where Big Mary had gone.

Distraught, Angelou went to Tolbrook's house to ask for help. But if she had ever thought there was a future with him, she quickly realized she had been kidding herself. He was furious that she had come to his home where he lived with his wife. He considered her nothing more than a common prostitute, and she then realized how naive she had been. "I had been stupid, again," she writes in *Gather Together in My Name*. "And stupidity had led me into a trap where I had lost my baby."[35]

Forcing herself to think calmly, she remembered the neighbor saying that Big Mary had a brother in another town called Bakersfield. With little money and dwindling hope, she boarded a bus that took her to Bakersfield, and she began asking people if they had seen a woman matching Big Mary's description. It was a long shot, however, because she did not have a last name or a description of Mary's brother.

Found at Last

Angelou did recall that although Big Mary did not drink often, one day a month she would go to a bar. (Angelou remembered, because on those days, someone else would watch the children.) Mary would walk to a bar and drink three bourbons from a large coffee cup. Angelou began going to all of the black bars in Bakersfield asking if they had seen such a woman.

Finally, one bartender recognized the description and gave her the location of Mary's brother's home. There she found Clyde,

Impossible Expectations

In *Gather Together in My Name*, Angelou writes about leaving San Francisco after Curley left her. She first visited her father's family in Los Angeles, hoping they would help her find the security she had dreamed of—dreams that had been fueled by unrealistic Hollywood romances. When the family in Los Angeles did not come through for her, she recalls being distraught:

> I was hurt because they didn't take me and my child to their bosom, and because I was a product of Hollywood upbringing and my own romanticism. On the silver screen they would have set me up in a cute little cottage with frangipani [flowering trees] and roses growing in the front yard. I would always wear pretty aprons and my son would play in the Little League. My husband would come home (he looked like Curley) and smoke his pipe in the den as I made cookies for the Boy Scouts meeting.

Maya Angelou, *Gather Together in My Name*. New York: Random House, 1974, p. 36.

playing outside by himself. Mary apologized, but insisted that she loved the little boy as her own, and begged Angelou to let him stay longer. Angelou refused, and not even waiting for Mary to pack Clyde's things, took her baby and left. She realized then that she had loved Clyde only as a little part of herself, instead of a person in his own right:

> Separate from my boundaries, I had not known before that he had and would have a life beyond being my son, my pretty baby, my cute doll, my charge. In the plowed farmyard near Bakersfield, I began to understand that uniqueness of the person. He was three and I was nineteen, and never again would I think of him as a beautiful appendage of myself.[36]

Troubadour Martin

Back in San Francisco, Angelou began job hunting again—this time determined that she and Clyde would be separated as seldom as possible. She got a job in a restaurant and met a man named Troubadour Martin. One day he approached her with an idea for a way to make money.

He offered her an easy job—one which she could do while staying at home with Clyde. Martin sold stolen goods—mostly women's dresses and suits. He needed a place that women could go to try on the clothing before they bought it. He would give Angelou a percentage of the money he made from sales. She agreed.

The job was, as Martin had promised, an easy one. She loved spending time reading during the day. She and Clyde went to movies and she loved reading to him. Never had she felt closer to her son. As time went on, she began thinking about Martin as a possible husband. He was kind and gentle, and as always, she wanted some stability in her life. But her experience with Troubadour Martin would show how desperate she had become.

Away from the Edge

From her experiences with her brother, Angelou could tell that Martin was a heroin user. She wondered if he would feel more comfortable about deepening their relationship if she offered to take heroin, too—just once. "One hit of heroin wouldn't make me an addict," she remembers reasoning. "And maybe if I shot it once, he'd know I didn't disapprove and our relationship would be closer."[37]

One evening, she pouted and asked Martin if he had another girlfriend. She wanted to know, she told him, because he seemed to have places to go that did not include her. He evaded her questions for awhile, but then agreed that she could come along with him. She found a babysitter for Clyde and took a ride with Martin.

He took her to a cheap hotel, where he got a key from the clerk. The room was filled with heroin users, in various stages of drug use. Martin forced her into the bathroom, rolled up his shirtsleeve, and made her watch as he filled a syringe with heroin and injected it into his arm. He offered her some, knowing that seeing heroin use up close would repulse her.

Maya witnessed the horrors of using heroin when she was with boyfriend Troubadour Martin. He made her vow to never use the drug, and she agreed.

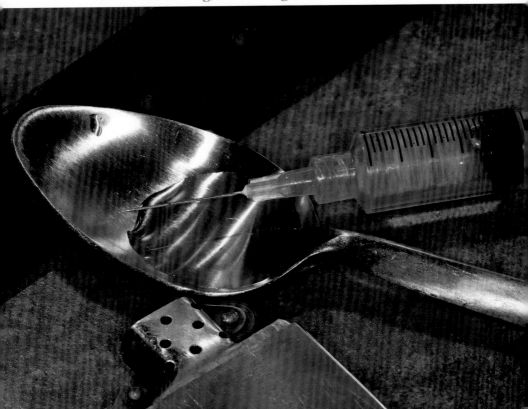

She realized quickly that he wanted to show her the horrors of addiction, so she would never become a user. He made her promise that she would never use drugs, and she agreed. Afterward she watched him as he slouched in the driver's seat of his car as he rested before taking her home. She realized then that he was in the grip of a terrible addiction and that he had just changed her life:

> I thought about the kindness of the man. I had wanted him before for the security I thought he'd give me. . . . No one had ever cared for me so much. He had exposed himself to me to teach me a lesson and I learned it. . . . I had walked the precipice and seen it all; and at the critical moment, one man's generosity had pushed me safely away from the edge.[38]

The next day, she decided that she and her son would go to live with her mother. She was not at all sure of what she was going to do with her life. But she had made a promise to Troubadour Martin, and she intended to keep it. She was going to work hard to make sure that the future for her and Clyde would be brighter.

Chapter 4

Taking Wing

When she returned to her mother's house, Angelou knew her days of using marijuana and being an irresponsible young mother were over. For the next two years she worked hard at two jobs—one in a real estate office and the other at a dress shop. Clyde was still away from her five days a week, since she was working days and evenings, and that was hard on both of them. But on her days off, she and Clyde would fill the time finding fun, inexpensive things to do—visiting the zoo, playing in the park, seeing a movie, or going to a museum.

"Life Was a Pleasure Ring"

Angelou also spent a lot of lunch hours in the Melrose Record Shop, which like many stores in those days allowed customers to open an album and listen to it on earphones before they decided to buy. She became familiar with different styles of music and found her tastes expanding. She loved listening to jazz—especially jazz artists like Sarah Vaughan, Nat King Cole, and Billie Holiday.

She gradually got to know the store's owner, a white woman named Louise Cox. Cox would ask her opinion of some of the music and often sought her advice on which jazz or gospel albums to feature in the store. Angelou later recalled being somewhat distrustful of Cox, for she had never had a close relationship with a white person. Nonetheless, when Cox offered her a job at the shop, she took it.

Maya spent a lot of time at the Melrose Record Shop in San Francisco, where she listened to jazz artists Nat King Cole (pictured), Sarah Vaughan, and Billie Holiday.

The job allowed her the freedom of not having to work a second job, and thus she was able to spend evenings with Clyde. Life became much more manageable for the young mother and her son. As she later wrote, "For months, life was a pleasure ring and we walked safely in its perimeter."[39]

Marriage

While working at the record store, Angelou got to be friendly with a customer—a Greek sailor-turned-electrician named Tosh Angelos. He loved music as much as she did, especially jazz. When he and Angelou began dating, she was thrilled to see how well he got along with Clyde.

But as her interest in Angelos increased, so did her mother's disapproval. She was not happy that the man was white, and that he was relatively poor. Worse, she predicted, Angelou would be caught in the middle of racial strife. "Think ahead," her mother ordered. "What the hell is he bringing you? The contempt of his people and the distrust of your own. That's a hell of a wedding gift."[40]

Even so, when Angelos proposed, Angelou accepted. She understood the reservations her mother had, but she believed it was best, for her and for Clyde. She quit her job and became a full-time homemaker and mother. "My life began to resemble a *Good Housekeeping* advertisement," she later wrote. "I cooked well-balanced meals and molded fabulous jello desserts. My floors were dangerous with daily applications of wax and our furniture slick with polish."[41]

Parting Ways

For a while, the marriage was fine. Angelos was a good father to Clyde, teaching him chess and playing ball with him. He helped with housework and was enthusiastic about Angelou continuing her dance lessons. But over time, there were signs that the marriage was not as perfect as she had hoped.

Angelos, though loving and caring to her and Clyde, was an introvert. He did not like most of her friends and preferred that they did not come to the house. But the thing that most angered her was his telling Clyde that there was no God. She had been raised in the church in Stamps and had always considered herself a Christian. Unwilling to challenge her husband openly, Angelou began sneaking out of the house on Sunday mornings and attending various black churches.

Things exploded one day after a representative of one of the churches called about Angelou becoming a member. She was not home at the time, and Angelos took the call. When she returned, Angelos was furious with her. Finally, Angelos told Angelou he was tired of being married, and the two parted ways in 1952.

Maya Angelou, Cuban Dancer

After her marriage ended, Angelou saw an advertisement that a nightclub called the Garden of Allah needed dancers. She responded and got the job. It was clear immediately that the customers loved her. Some of them turned out to be the owners of one of San Francisco's most famous nightclubs—the Purple Onion. They invited her to a private party after she was done performing.

During the evening, Angelou felt a little ill at ease. And she became angry when Jorie, one of the Purple Onion singers, made what Angelou felt was a racist remark about calypso music (sung by blacks in Caribbean countries). Without really thinking, Angelou launched into a calypso song, which astonished the partygoers. The owners of the Purple Onion immediately offered her a job singing calypso.

Angelou's calypso career began in the 1950s when she recorded an album titled Miss Calypso.

The idea was to introduce her as a Cuban (which of course, she was not) and she would need a more exotic name. She told them her brother had always called her Maya and that worked. The last name of Angelos sounded too Italian, so they changed it a little to Angelou. That day, Maya Angelou was born.

She quickly went to work learning more than a dozen calypso songs. And, she later explained, it was difficult to keep the words straight:

> I was hired at the club as a singer, but the songs had many refrains and such complex rhythms that often I got lost in the plot and forgot the lyrics. So, when the words eluded me, I would admit my poor memory and add that if the audience would bear with me I would dance.[42]

A Job Offer

When Angelou was not working, she spent time creating new material. Since her days in Stamps when she did not speak, she had been writing poetry. Now she threw herself into writing more—and creating new calypso songs for her act. She also began taking singing lessons to make her voice stronger. Her teacher was Frederick Wilkerson, whom she affectionately called "Uncle Wilkie." He taught her ways to use her voice so that she could sing loudly but not injure her vocal cords, as she was in danger of doing.

It was during this time that she saw George Gershwin's Broadway hit, an all-black opera called *Porgy and Bess*. She was astonished at how wonderful it was. She writes, "I remained in my seat after the curtain fell and allowed people to climb over my knees to reach the aisle. *Porgy and Bess* had shown me the greatest array of Negro talent I had ever seen."[43]

She was even more astonished months later when she was offered a chance to join the traveling production of the play, playing the part of Ruby—the character she had most enjoyed. It would be a year-long commitment, for the cast would be traveling throughout the world, and she was concerned about leaving Clyde, now ten years old. But he would be with his grandmother, whom he adored, and with whom he was now very comfortable. He would be loved and taken care of, Angelou knew. And what exciting stories she would have to tell him when she returned!

Around the World

So between 1954 and 1955 Angelou toured Greece, Spain, Russia, Italy—places she had only read about. As she recalled later, Angelou was breathless to see the city of Verona, Italy, where Shakespeare's *Romeo and Juliet* took place:

> I was really in Italy. Not Maya Angelou, the person of pretentions and ambitions, but me, Marguerite Johnson, who had read about Verona and the sad lovers while growing up in a dusty Southern village poorer and more tragic than the historic town in which I now stood.[44]

Starring in Porgy *and* Bess, *Angelou traveled the world with the production. She visited places she had only read about in books—such as Italy, Russia, and Spain.*

It was thrilling, too, to be part of a production that so moved audiences throughout the world. Everywhere they went, they were mobbed and treated as stars. She felt an exhilaration she had never experienced before. But while *Porgy and Bess* was beyond everything she had hoped for, she was getting uneasy about leaving Clyde for so long. His letters to her always seemed sad, and in each one he asked when she would be home. Finally, she got a letter from her mother, saying that she was taking a job in Las Vegas as a dealer. She would no longer be able to watch Clyde. Even more disturbing, her mother said, Clyde had developed a rash that the doctors were unable to cure. Angelou needed to come home immediately.

Never Again

When she finally arrived back in San Francisco, Angelou was astonished at the change in nine-year-old Clyde. "The loquacious, beautiful and bubbling child I had left had disappeared," she later wrote. "In his place was a rough-skinned shy boy who hung his head when spoken to and refused to maintain eye contact even when I held his chin and asked, 'Look at me.'"[45]

Guilty, certain that her absence had caused her son's terrible rash and deep sadness, Angelou did not know what to do. She began to think that she would be better off dead. One afternoon she went to her former voice teacher, Uncle Wilkie. He would not let her feel sorry for herself. Instead, he made her write down all the things she could be thankful for. Being able to write, to dance, being thankful that she had a son who loved her—all of these were things she should focus on.

She realized he was right. She went home and promised Clyde that she would never leave him again. If she left, he would come, too. She got a new job in the city at a theatrical agency. Clyde became more secure each passing day. He no longer checked where she was in the house, fearful of being left again. His rash cleared up, and he became more confident. He even informed his mother he no longer wanted to be named Clyde, but rather Guy. She and the rest of the family willingly honored his wishes. Things were getting better.

"When I'm Writing, Everything Shuts Down"

The routine Angelou follows when she is writing is the same, whether she is working on an inaugural poem or a volume of her autobiography. In an interview with Carol Sarler for the *Sunday Times Magazine*, she explains in detail various aspects of that routine:

> When I'm writing, everything shuts down. I get up at five, take a shower and I don't use the [expensive floral soap]—I don't want that sensual gratification. I get in my car and drive to a hotel room. . . . [I] ask them to take everything off the walls, so there's me, the Bible, *Roget's Thesaurus*, and some good, dry sherry and I'm at work by 6:30. I write on the bed lying down—one elbow is darker than the other, really black from leaning on it—and I write in longhand on yellow pads. Once into it, all disbelief is suspended, it's beautiful. I hate to go, but I've set for myself 12:30 as the time to leave, because after that . . . it becomes stuff I'm going to edit out anyway. . . .
>
> If April is the cruellest month, eight o'clock at night is the cruellest hour because that's when I start to edit. and all that pretty stuff I've written gets axed out. So if I've written 10 or 12 pages in six hours, it'll end up as three or four if I'm lucky.

Quoted in Carol Sarler, "A Life in the Day of Maya Angelou," *Sunday Times Magazine*, December 27, 1987.

The Writing Life

The 1950s ended, and Angelou shifted her interest from entertaining to writing. She had always written poetry, but never felt sure of herself. She met John Killens, a talented black author, when he came to California. He had written a novel called *Youngblood* and was currently writing the screenplay so it could become a movie. She showed some of her writing to Killens, and he was enthusiastic. He told her she had promise, but if she really wanted to grow as a writer, she should consider moving to New York. There was a talented group of black writers there who had formed the Harlem Writers' Guild to help one another with their writing.

She and Guy (now fourteen) got an apartment in the city, and Angelou became a new member of the Harlem Writers' Guild. It was scary reading some of her work aloud to the group. She wrote years later:

> The blood pounded in my ears but not enough to drown the skinny sound of my voice. My hands shook so that I had to lay the pages in my lap, but that was not a good solution due to the tricks my knees were playing. They lifted voluntarily, pulling my heels off the floor like disturbed Jello.[46]

She hoped that she would get some positive feedback on her work, but she was disappointed. One of the members, an editor and poet named John Henrik Clarke, was quite critical, saying he found her work rather lifeless. Angelou was humiliated, although Clarke came up to her later and told her that the group was glad to have her there. He insisted that she had a story to tell, and that she could benefit from the group's help. Rewriting something over and over, he explained, was simply a part of the writing process.

That was an important lesson for her, and she realized that someday she might be able to earn a living as a writer, but she had a long way to go before that would happen. For the time being, she would write as a hobby and earn money as an entertainer.

Meeting King

The 1960s was a time of great excitement for many African Americans. The civil rights movement was gaining energy, especially under the leadership of a young minister named Martin Luther King Jr. King and his Southern Christian Leadership Conference (SCLC) advocated nonviolent protests against racism and segregation.

When King came to New York to speak at a Harlem church, Angelou and her friend, an actor named Godfrey Cambridge, went to

During the civil rights movement, Angelou was hired by Martin Luther King Jr.'s SCLC organization to coordinate volunteer efforts by college students and fund-raising.

hear him. Afterward they were speechless. Both agreed that they needed to do something to support King, and they decided to create a theater presentation and donate the proceeds to the SCLC. They eventually decided it would be a sort of variety show with various black entertainers. Called *Cabaret for Freedom*, the show played the entire summer of 1960 to packed audiences. The last song each night was "Lift Ev'ry Voice and Sing," which, since her eighth grade graduation, had always had a very special meaning to Angelou.

Interestingly, after the show closed, Angelou was contacted by the SCLC. They were impressed by her skills at organizing the event and offered her a position in the organization. The job would

Most of All, a Human Being

In an extensive interview with Washington, D.C.'s Academy of Achievement, Angelou explains that although Martin Luther King Jr. was a great man, it is important to remember that he was a human being, too. Knowing that makes his accomplishments more profound. Angelou says:

> He had a sense of humor which was wonderful. It is very dangerous to make a person larger than life because, then, young men and women are tempted to believe, well, if he was that great, he's inaccessible, and I can never try to be that or emulate that or achieve that. The truth is, Martin Luther King was a human being with a brilliant mind, a powerful heart, and insight, and courage and also with a sense of humor. So he was accessible. . . . Dr. King was really humble so that he was accessible to everybody. The smallest child could come up to him, the most powerful person could come up to him, he never changed.

Quoted in "Maya Angelou Interview," Academy of Achievement. www.achievement.org/autodoc/page/ang0int-1.

be coordinating volunteer efforts by college students and helping with fund-raising. Proud to work in King's organization to further the cause of civil rights, she eagerly accepted.

Vasumzi Make

Besides working at the SCLC, Angelou continued to write. She had become engaged to Thomas Allen, a retired bail bondsman, although as time went on, she was disappointed that he did not seem to care about her civil rights work. When she met a South African activist named Vasumzi (Vus) Make in 1961, she fell instantly in love.

Make had been exiled from South Africa for fighting against the repressive white government there. He was visiting New York to raise money for his cause. His work was exciting, and Angelou longed to help him. She broke off her engagement with Allen when Make proposed to her. They soon married and left for London, where they would have a honeymoon and where Make was scheduled to take part in a conference.

Although she was proud of the work Make was doing for freeing African people, she was less happy about the restrictions he put on her own life. When they returned to New York, he wanted Angelou to be an African wife, which meant she should be subservient to her husband. He did not want her to work, but rather spend her time keeping their apartment clean. As she wrote later in her autobiography *The Heart of a Woman*, he had high expectations:

> Vus was particular. He checked on my progress. Sometimes he pulled the sofa away from the wall to see if possibly I had missed a layer of dust. If he found his suspicions confirmed his response would wither me. He would drop his eyes and shake his head, his face saddened with disappointment. . . . I was unemployed but I had never worked so hard in all my life.[47]

The Blacks

Later in 1960, Angelou was approached about doing a play called *The Blacks*, by French playwright Jean Genet. After reading it, she was not terribly impressed, for it bothered her that a white European was writing about people that he had no way of really knowing. She also knew that Make would not want her to perform. But after reading through the script, he surprised her. He believed the play could possibly raise social awareness about black issues. He urged her to take the part when it was offered.

Featuring great actors, such as Lou Gossett Jr., Cicely Tyson, and James Earl Jones, the play had an all-star cast. Using black actors for all parts—black and white alike—it showed the constant struggle blacks endured because of white meanness. The play was an off-Broadway hit.

Angelou's experience in *The Blacks* did not end well, however. She had agreed to write two songs for the play, but the producers refused to pay her. Furious and aware that the irony of the situation mirrored the play's theme (the unfair treatment of blacks by whites) Angelou decided to take a stand and quit.

Angelou starred in French playwright Jean Genet's The Blacks *alongside great actors such as Cicely Tyson and James Earl Jones. The play was an off-Broadway hit.*

Moving to Egypt

For months, Make had been careless about the family's finances. Bills were ignored and the rent was far overdue. When Angelou came home one day to see an eviction notice on their front door, Make said he would take care of everything. He moved them into a New York hotel and left for Africa. After a few weeks, he wired Angelou and Guy the tickets so they could join him there.

They settled in Cairo, Egypt, where Make could continue his work, gaining support for South African freedom. But once again, Make forbade her to work outside the home, and once again, their finances were in shambles. Guy's tuition was unpaid, and the family received notices to return furnishings they had purchased for their Cairo home.

A Deteriorating Marriage

Although her husband did not want her to work, Angelou decided to look for a job anyway. She finally found employment at an English-language news weekly called the *Arab Observer*. Even though she had no experience, a friend who worked there stretched the truth a little, saying she had done reporting in the past. As a result, she was made associate editor. Angelou recalls being both excited and frightened at getting such an important job with almost no qualifications. "I felt," she writes, "as though I had fallen into a deep trench with steep muddy sides."[48]

But when she told Make, he was furious with her for not being a good African wife, shouting, "You took a job without consulting me? Are you a man?"[49] In her autobiography, Angelou writes that as Make was raging at her, she realized that she was no longer in love with him. She had been attracted to his brilliance and his courage in fighting injustice, but "the man standing over me, venting his fury, was no longer my love."[50] In addition, she had begun to suspect that Make was cheating on her. It was time, she decided, to think about ending the marriage.

Even though she would be raising a teenage son alone and she was far, far from home, she knew being on her own was something she could do. She was getting better at making decisions, and she knew that she and Guy would be able to survive. She and Make stayed together for awhile after that argument, especially so Guy could finish his last year of high school. She continued to work at the *Arab Observer*—a job she was beginning to love. Once Guy graduated in 1962, however, she and Make finally parted—as friends.

Instead of returning to the United States, Angelou and Guy decided to remain in Africa for awhile. There were many things they wanted to see.

Chapter 5

The Do-It-All Woman

The plan, after leaving Cairo, was to visit West Africa. They would go to Ghana first. Having recently won its independence from Britain, Ghana had a world-class university that Guy wanted to attend. Angelou would get him settled, and then go on to visit Liberia.

A Very Different Place

Their first few days in Ghana were amazing. They enjoyed walking through the streets of Accra, Ghana's capital. Never had they been in a place where blacks were the majority and also in charge. In her autobiography, *The Heart of a Woman*, Angelou recalls how strange it was to see blacks doing jobs they were not allowed to do in the United States:

> Three black men walked passed us wearing airline uniforms, visored caps, white pants and jackets whose shoulders bristled with epaulettes. Black pilots? Black captains? It was 1962. In our country, the cradle of democracy, whose anthem boasted "the land of the free, the home of the brave," the only black men in our airports fueled planes, cleaned cabins, loaded food or were skycaps, racing the pavement for tips.[51]

But Angelou's excitement to be in such an interesting city evaporated a few days after they arrived. While out with some new friends, Guy was injured in an automobile accident. In addition to a broken arm and leg, he had a broken neck. And while he survived the accident, Guy had to remain in the hospital for a month and would need to recuperate at home for three months after that.

African Roots

It was clear that she would need a job in Ghana so that she could pay for Guy's care at the hospital as well as his long recuperation time at home. There were a large number of black Americans in Ghana, and they rallied around Angelou during this difficult time. Julian Mayfield, a friend whom she had known from the Harlem Writers' Guild, helped her get a job in the Theater Department at the University of Ghana. The university also found her a house she could stay in for three months, that of a professor who was on a leave of absence.

Besides working and caring for Guy, Angelou was determined to fit in to her new surroundings. She made a decision to immerse herself in this culture that was new to her. She put her "American" clothing away and began to wear the long, colorful gowns and head wraps worn by the women of Ghana. She learned several new languages, including Fanti, so she could make new friends. She even learned to cook traditional African dishes.

Angelou also wanted to learn more about some of the unpleasant things that were part of the history of all African Americans whose ancestors had been brought to America as slaves. There was a town on Ghana's coast where Africans had been imprisoned by slave traders before being transported to the United States. She visited the town, called Cape Coast, and recalled later that she could almost visualize the scene, though it had occurred centuries before:

> I allowed the shapes to come to my imagination: children passed tied together by ropes and chains, tears abashed, stumbling in dull exhaustion, then women, hair uncombed, bodies gritted with sand, and sagging in defeat. Men, muscles without memory, minds dimmed, plodding, leaving

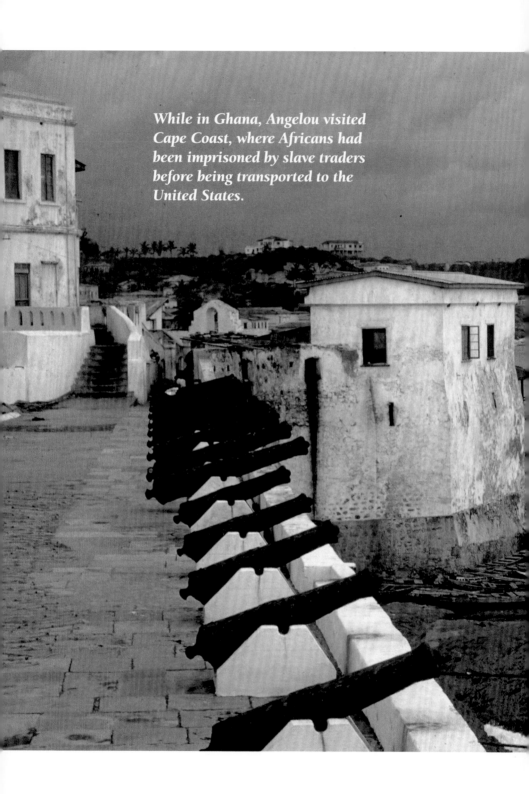

While in Ghana, Angelou visited Cape Coast, where Africans had been imprisoned by slave traders before being transported to the United States.

bloodied footprints in the dirt. . . . None of them cried, or yelled, or bellowed. No moans came from them. They lived in a mute territory, dead to feelings and protest.[52]

Civil Rights in Africa

At the same time that she was learning more about the unpleasant history of Ghana and the slave trade, Angelou followed news of the civil rights movement back in the United States. She and other African Americans visiting Ghana read about Martin Luther King Jr.'s upcoming march on Washington, D.C., planned for August 27, 1963. Angelou and many of her friends visiting Ghana had become disenchanted with King's insistence on nonviolence. They believed that nothing would come of the struggle unless blacks in America became more forceful about their demands for equality.

However, they thought it was necessary to show their support for King's march. They planned their own march against the U.S. embassy in Accra at the same time as King's march. Because of the time difference, the demonstration in Accra started at midnight. For hours she and about one hundred other African Americans marched and sang songs, and as the sun began to come up, Angelou had an unsettling realization. As she wrote later, she was struck by the fact that while she and the other Americans had believed that they could find their true home in Africa by escaping the racism in the United States, that really was not possible:

> Many of us had begun to realize in Africa that the Stars and Stripes was our flag and our only flag, and that knowledge was almost too painful to bear. We could physically return to Africa, find jobs, learn languages, even marry and remain on African soil all our lives, but we were born in the United States, and it was the United States which had rejected, enslaved, exploited, and denied us. It was the United States which held the graves of our grandmothers and grandfathers. It was in the United States, under conditions that were too bizarre to detail, that those same ancestors had worked and dreamed of "a better day, by and by."[53]

Back to America

Not long after that, Angelou met up with Malcolm X. She had met him in the United States when she lived in New York. Malcolm X had strongly differed from the nonviolent policies of King and urged that blacks should separate themselves from white Americans, no matter how sympathetic they seemed to the cause of civil rights. Whites, he had warned, could not be trusted, ever.

But by 1964, when he came to Ghana, Malcolm X had changed his ideas. He no longer believed in keeping the races separate. In fact, he now believed that equality between blacks and whites was possible. After he left Ghana, he continued to correspond with Angelou and others about his plans. One of his goals was to raise the issue at the United Nations (UN) in New York. He hoped that by appealing to representatives of the world's nations, the UN could vote to officially condemn the racism in the United States.

Malcolm X even promised Angelou a job when she decided to return to the United States. He was forming the Organization of

"The Great Thing About Being the Son of Maya Angelou"

In an online chat on the African American Literature Book Club Web site, Angelou's son Guy Johnson—now a successful fiction writer—talks about growing up with a famous mother. Johnson says:

> It took me quite some time to discover that I wanted to write. The great thing about being the son of Maya Angelou is that I had the good fortune to grow up around some of the greatest black artists, dancers, singers, musicians, and actors of our time. My mother was in *The Blacks* in 1960, in that cast were Ossie Davis, Ruby Dee, James Earl Jones . . . and there were so many more I can't even remember. In terms of musicians, Billie Holiday, Clifford Brown, Eric Dolphy, et cetera. And on the political side she headed Martin Luther King's Southern Christian Leadership Conference, so of course I met Martin Luther King. Muhammad Ali met Malcolm X for the first time at my mother's house. So I would say I had the great fortune of living with one of the most inspiring creative people, and she was my mother.

Guy Johnson, online chat, African American Literature Book Club, December 10, 1998, http://aalbc.com/authors/guyjohnson.htm.

Angelou and her son Guy Johnson at the National Black Arts Festival in 2005.

Malcolm X promised Angelou a job in his organization when she left Ghana; however, two days after her arrival he was killed.

Afro-American Unity (OAAU), and hoped that she would become one of its coordinators—using the same organizational skills she had developed while working for the Southern Christian Leadership Conference years before. The idea was very appealing to her. Guy was now twenty years old—a grown man, a graduate of the University of Ghana, who no longer needed her in the same way as he had before. Angelou returned to the United States in February 1965. Two days after she arrived home, however, Malcolm X was assassinated in New York. Her work for the OAAU was over before it had even begun.

Throwing Herself into Writing

After Malcolm X's murder, Angelou decided that political work was not for her. Instead, in the late 1960s, she turned inward, and began writing. She was offered a position at the University of California, Los Angeles as a guest lecturer, which afforded her a steady paycheck while she experimented with new types of writing. While she had written song lyrics, newspaper articles, and some poetry in the past, she felt it was important to try different ways to explain what she had seen and experienced—both in Africa and America.

She wrote a two-act play called *The Least of These*, and later, ten one-hour programs for National Educational Television, which ran as a series in 1968. Called *Black, Blues, Black*, the series documents the role that African culture has had on life in the United States. In 1969 she also recorded an album of her poetry.

Some of Angelou's friends thought she should write the story of her life. One friend went so far as to talk to an editor at Random House, a book publisher, about the idea. The editor, Robert Loomis, called Angelou several times about writing her autobiography, but each time she politely turned him down. Interestingly, however, she finally agreed—having been tricked into it, as she later explained:

> Then, I'm sure he [Loomis] talked to [my friend James] Baldwin because he used a ploy which I'm not proud to say I haven't gained control of yet. He called and said, "Miss Angelou,

it's been nice talking to you. I'm rather glad you decided not to write an autobiography, because to write an autobiography, as literature, is the most difficult thing anyone can do." I said, "I'll do it." . . . The minute someone says I can't, all my energy goes up and I say, what? What?[54]

"It Was Special and Unique"

In 1970 the first volume of Angelou's autobiography, *I Know Why the Caged Bird Sings*, was published. It chronicles her life as a child in Stamps, all the way to age sixteen, with the birth of her son. The book was an instant success, not only in the United States, but also around the world. It was the first book by an African American woman to ever appear on the *New York Times* best seller list. Not only was it popular with readers, but the book also received critical acclaim, too. It was nominated for the National Book Award.

Although he was confident the book would be very good, editor Loomis was highly impressed at the honest tone of the book. "It was special and unique," he later recalled. "She wrote with such anger and disgust at the prejudice [she endured], but did not have any of that bitterness, which ruins a lot of writers."[55]

Soon after finishing that book, Angelou completed a book of poems, *Just Give Me a Cool Drink of Water 'fore I Diiie*, which was nominated for the Pulitzer Prize in 1970. Not long afterward, she began working on a screenplay called *Georgia, Georgia*. The theme of the screenplay was interracial marriage and the complex problems between black men and black women. *Georgia, Georgia* broke new ground, too, being the first screenplay by an African American woman ever to be made into a movie.

Growing

No matter what type of writing she attempted, Angelou continued to challenge herself to try something new with each project, to expand her abilities. For instance, in *Georgia, Georgia*, she was determined to write the musical score for the movie—although she had no formal musical training, as she explained later to one interviewer:

Angelou with a copy of her autobiography I Know Why the Caged Bird Sings, which was published in 1970 and appeared on the New York Times best seller list.

I'm not a trained musician, but I can hear very well, so in order to do the score I had to sing all the parts into a tape recorder. I'd sing the piano part, sing the first violin part, the second violin, cello, and bass. Then I'd put the whole score in a shopping bag for the transcriber.[56]

It was during the production of that same movie that she decided she wanted to learn the art of making movies, too. If she were going to write stories that would be made into movies, then she realized she would love to be able to direct them herself. To do that, of course, she would need to have a command of the techniques moviemakers use to bring the stories to life.

After the shooting for *Georgia, Georgia* was complete, she later returned to Stockholm, Sweden—where *Georgia, Georgia* had been made—to learn about moviemaking. "I . . . took an eight-month course in cinematography," she explained to one interviewer. "I crammed it in in a little less than two months. Since I'll be directing, I want to know what the camera can do."[57]

Accolades as a Performer

During the 1970s, Angelou grew as a performer, too. Although she had done very well in the traveling company of *Porgy and Bess* as a young woman, and in *The Blacks* while she lived in New York in 1960, it had been years since she had acted. In 1973 when she was offered the part of First Lady Mary Todd Lincoln's dressmaker in a two-person play called *Look Away*, she eagerly took it. To her great delight, she was nominated for a Tony Award for her performance.

When author Alex Haley was working on an adaptation of his book *Roots* as a miniseries for television in 1977, Angelou hoped to direct one segment. However, time and budget constraints made it necessary for the project to hire directors with more experience. She was, however, offered the role of Kunta Kinte's grandmother in the series, which she accepted. She told interviewer Curt Davis that not only was she nominated for an Emmy Award for that role, but that she also became an instant celebrity:

Angelou's Georgia, Georgia was the first screenplay to be written by an African-American woman that was made into a movie.

After it was done, I found that people knew me. I walked down the street, especially the first month. I've written five books, I can't say how many plays, movie scripts, music, and poetry, and so forth. I walk down the street and people say, "You're the actress in *Roots*. What's your name again, and what have you been doing all this time?[58]

Angelou was nominated for an Emmy for the role of Kunta Kinte's grandmother in the miniseries **Roots.**

Adding Titles

Even as her performances were being applauded, Angelou continued writing her life story during the 1970s. *Gather Together in My Name* was published in 1974, and a third autobiographical volume, *Singin' and Swingin' and Gettin' Merry Like Christmas*, was published in 1976. She later admitted it was difficult writing these, especially *Gather Together*, because there were so many painful and private aspects of her family's life that she had to deal with. In 1975 she sat down with a reporter and explained how her family had decided it was appropriate for her to publish that second volume of her autobiography, even though it was so much more difficult to write than the first one:

> It was worse [than writing *I Know Why the Caged Bird Sings*]. *Gather Together* deals with unsavory parts of my past. I'm now a Chubb Fellow at Yale University and Distinguished Professor at three universities in the country, and to admit some of the things I've admitted was very painful.

> I called my son, my mother, and my brother . . . and I said, "This is what I want to do. I want to say to young people, You may encounter many defeats, but you must not be defeated." Then I read them the salient chapters, and my mother said, "Write it." My brother said, "Send it in." My son got up . . . and said, "You're so great, Mom. Please tell it."[59]

A Lifetime Appointment

The 1970s and 1980s were busy decades. Angelou wrote more books of poetry as well as the final two volumes of her autobiography—*The Heart of a Woman* and *A Song Flung Up to Heaven*. In 1981 Angelou was awarded a lifetime position as a professor at Wake Forest University in Winston-Salem, North Carolina. Although she had lectured at colleges in the past, it was not the same as teaching a course—and she soon realized how much she enjoyed teaching.

She has found that although she never went to college, she has a great deal to offer to young people. Wake Forest has been good for her, she says, and the students are eager to learn. "I see all those little faces and big eyes," she says. "Black and white. They look like sparrows in the nest. They look up, with their mouths wide open and I try to drop in everything I know."[60]

Her obligation to Wake Forest has only been to teach one class per semester and that has allowed her to work on other projects. In 1994 she tried her hand at writing a children's book, called *My Painted House, My Friendly Chicken, and Me*. That same year she was approached by Tom Feelings, an award-winning artist. Feelings was working on a children's book of poetry—aimed especially at young African American children, and he wanted to include poetry by Angelou. She was thrilled to be part of the project, and her poem, "I Love the Look of Words," from the book is popular with children throughout the United States.

Celebrating Her Eightieth Birthday

On April 4, 2008, Maya Angelou turned eighty years old, and her current hometown of Winston-Salem, North Carolina, held a special celebration for her. She was thrilled to learn that the mayor had proclaimed a new name for the intersection of First and Liberty streets in the city, to be known thereafter as "Dr. Maya Angelou Way."

Even more moving, she admitted, was the gathering of performers at the plaza who sang special African songs, and the more than four hundred well-wishers who came to cheer for Angelou. "This is what we look like at our very best," she told them all. "Imagine, just imagine, these children singing African songs to an old African-American woman in Winston-Salem, North Carolina. . . . Thank you for having enough courage to come out and be somebody."

Quoted in Jim Sparks, "A Unifier of People: A Mixed Crowd Sings, Dances in Celebration," *Winston-Salem Journal*, April 20, 2008.

Hallelujah! The Welcome Table

In 2002 Angelou tried another new project: a cookbook. Angelou has always loved to cook. Talk show host Oprah Winfrey, who has been a friend of hers for many years, urged her to write a cookbook. Oprah, who has eaten many times in Angelou's kitchen, told her that some of her recipes, along with stories about the special food she makes, would give people a chance to learn about her in a whole new way. The result, called *Hallelujah! The Welcome Table*, contains recipes and stories from Angelou's childhood in Stamps, Arkansas, to the more exotic places around the world where Angelou has lived.

One of the most poignant stories accompanies the recipe for caramel cake, which was Momma's specialty. It was famous throughout Stamps for its rich texture. But the reason that caramel cake is special to Angelou is far more personal. The story is from the time she did not speak, in the years after she was raped. While her muteness was pretty much accepted by the people in Stamps, there was a new teacher named Miss Williams in their elementary school who did not know Angelou. She demanded that Angelou speak, and when she did not, Miss Williams slapped her across the face. Momma, who almost always took a teacher's side of any argument, came to her granddaughter's defense. She marched up to the school and slapped Miss Williams across the face. "Now, Sister, nobody has the right to hit nobody in the face," Momma told the teacher. "So I am wrong this time, but I'm teaching a lesson."[61] That evening, Momma made a caramel cake, though she was silent about the reason. It was Uncle Willie who explained why. "This cake can't pay you for being slapped in the face," he said. "Momma made it just to tell you how much we love you and how precious you are."[62]

"People Won't See the Likes of Her Again"

As Maya Angelou turned eighty years old in April 2008, she showed little evidence of slowing down. Although she is a bit unsteady on her feet and uses a cane, she is still a dominant 6-foot-tall (1.8m)

presence in any room. She insists she has no plans to retire. She is still very happy in her role as a professor at Wake Forest, and there is a waiting list for students wanting to take her class.

Beyond that, she has other plans about which she is very excited She hosts a weekly radio show on the Oprah and Friends channel. She is working on the lyrics for a new opera by composer Richard Danielpour. In 2007 she began composing some country music, a genre long dominated by white musicians.

She continues to travel, speaking and performing around the United States. Reading poetry, telling stories, singing, and even dancing a bit—she delights audiences wherever she goes. "I saw Maya a few months ago in Minneapolis," says William G. Jones, a retired

At eighty years old, Angelou has no plans to retire. She is happy in her role as professor at Wake Forest University, host of her own radio show, and composing music.

auto worker. "She is amazing, and I don't say that lightly. The hall was packed, but she connected with everybody. She made us all smile—it felt like she was talking just to us, one at a time. And when she does that little dance step up there—it's like she's twenty instead of eighty. She's got a gift, a rare gift. People won't see the likes of her again, not for a long, long time."[63]

Introduction: A Terrifying Honor

1. Quoted in *Jet*, "Blacks Play Biggest Role in Clinton Inauguration," *Jet*, February 8, 1993, p. 5.

2. Quoted in *People*, "Moment of Creation," *People*, January 18, 1993, p. 62.

3. Quoted in *People*, "Moment of Creation," p. 62.

Chapter 1: A Childhood in Stamps

4. Quoted in Jeffrey M. Elliot, ed., *Conversations with Maya Angelou*. Jackson: University Press of Mississippi, 1989, p. 87.

5. Quoted in Elliot, *Conversations with Maya Angelou*, p. 4.

6. Maya Angelou, interview by Bill Moyers, *Creativity with Bill Moyers: Maya Angelou*, video, directed by David Grubin. New York: WNET, 1982.

7. Quoted in Elliot, *Conversations with Maya Angelou*, p. 87.

8. Maya Angelou, *I Know Why the Caged Bird Sings*. New York: Random House, 1969, p. 18.

9. Maya Angelou, interview by Academy of Achievement, "Maya Angelou Interview," Academy of Achievement, January 22, 1997, www.achievement.org/autodoc/printmember/ang0int-1.

10. Angelou, *I Know Why the Caged Bird Sings*, p. 21.

11. Angelou, *I Know Why the Caged Bird Sings*, p. 21.

12. Angelou, *I Know Why the Caged Bird Sings*, p. 51.

13. Angelou, *I Know Why the Caged Bird Sings*, pp. 4–5.

14. Angelou, *I Know Why the Caged Bird Sings*, p. 57.

15. Angelou, *I Know Why the Caged Bird Sings*, p. 58.

16. Angelou, *I Know Why the Caged Bird Sings*, p. 84.

Chapter 2: Turning Points

17. Angelou, interview by Academy of Achievement, "Maya Angelou Interview."

18. Angelou, interview by Moyers, *Creativity with Bill Moyers: Maya Angelou.*

19. Quoted in Elliot, *Conversations with Maya Angelou*, p. 168.

20. Charles Dickens, *A Tale of Two Cities.* New York: Watts [no date], p. 3.

21. Angelou, interview by Moyers, *Creativity with Bill Moyers: Maya Angelou.*

22. Angelou, *I Know Why the Caged Bird Sings*, p. 94.

23. Angelou, *I Know Why the Caged Bird Sings*, p. 98.

24. Angelou, *I Know Why the Caged Bird Sings*, p. 170.

25. Angelou, *I Know Why the Caged Bird Sings*, p. 179.

26. Angelou, *I Know Why the Caged Bird Sings*, p. 104.

27. Angelou, *I Know Why the Caged Bird Sings*, p. 249.

28. Angelou, *I Know Why the Caged Bird Sings*, p. 256.

29. Angelou, *I Know Why the Caged Bird Sings*, p. 276.

Chapter 3: Out on Her Own

30. Maya Angelou, *Gather Together in My Name.* New York: Bantam, 1974, pp. 3–4.

31. Angelou, *Gather Together in My Name*, p. 27.

32. Angelou, *Gather Together in My Name*, p. 75.

33. Angelou, *Gather Together in My Name*, pp. 95–96.

34. Angelou, *Gather Together in My Name*, p. 171.

35. Angelou, *Gather Together in My Name*, p. 189.

36. Angelou, *Gather Together in My Name*, p. 195.

37. Angelou, *Gather Together in My Name*, p. 210.

38. Angelou, *Gather Together in My Name*, p. 215.

Chapter 4: Taking Wing

39. Maya Angelou, *Singin' and Swingin' and Gettin' Merry Like Christmas*. New York: Random House, 1976, p. 15.

40. Angelou, *Singin' and Swingin'*, p. 30.

41. Angelou, *Singin' and Swingin'*, pp. 31–32.

42. Angelou, *Singin' and Swingin'*, p. 100.

43. Angelou, *Singin' and Swingin'*, p. 127.

44. Angelou, *Singin' and Swingin'*, p. 157.

45. Angelou, *Singin' and Swingin'*, p. 257.

46. Maya Angelou, *The Heart of a Woman*. New York: Bantam, 1982, p. 42.

47. Angelou, *The Heart of a Woman*, p. 166.

48. Angelou, *The Heart of a Woman*, p. 266.

49. Angelou, *The Heart of a Woman*, p. 269.

50. Angelou, *The Heart of a Woman*, p. 270.

Chapter 5: The Do-It-All Woman

51. Angelou, *The Heart of a Woman*, p. 307.

52. Maya Angelou, *The Collected Biographies of Maya Angelou*. New York: Modern Library, 2004, pp. 963–64.

53. Angelou, *The Collected Biographies of Maya Angelou*, p. 987.

54. Quoted in Elliot, *Conversations with Maya Angelou*, p. 151.

55. Quoted in Gregg Hitt, "Maya Angelou," *Winston-Salem* (NC) *Journal*, December 1987.

56. Quoted in Elliot, *Conversations with Maya Angelou*, p. 137.

57. Quoted in Elliot, *Conversations with Maya Angelou*, p. 13.

58. Quoted in Elliot, *Conversations with Maya Angelou*, p. 71.

59. Quoted in Carol Benson, "Interview with Maya Angelou," *Writers Digest*, January 1975, p. 19.

60. Quoted in Bob Minzesheimer, "Angelou Celebrates Her Life," *USA Today,* March 27, 2008, p. D1.

61. Quoted in Maya Angelou, *Hallelujah! The Welcome Table: A Lifetime of Memories with Recipes*. New York: Random House, 2004, p. 16.

62. Quoted in Angelou, *Hallelujah! The Welcome Table*, p. 17.

63. William G. Jones, personal interview by the author, April 3, 2008, Minneapolis, MN.

1928

Maya Angelou is born in St. Louis, Missouri, on April 4.

1930

Maya and Bailey are sent to Stamps, Arkansas, to live with their father's mother, Annie Henderson.

1935

Maya is raped by her mother's boyfriend, Mr. Freeman, in St. Louis. That same year, she and Bailey return to Stamps.

1940

Maya graduates from the eighth grade. Afterward, she and Bailey go to live with their mother in San Francisco, California.

1945

Maya graduates from high school; her son Clyde (later called Guy) is born.

1949

Angelou and Tosh Angelos marry.

1952

Angelou and Tosh Angelos divorce.

1954

Angelou joins the touring company of *Porgy and Bess*.

1959

Angelou begins civil rights work at Martin Luther King Jr.'s Southern Christian Leadership Conference.

1960

Angelou and Vasumzi Make marry; she performs in *The Blacks*.

1961

Angelou, Make, and Guy move to Cairo, Egypt.

1962

Angelou and Make divorce; she and Guy move to Ghana.

1968

Angelou writes *Black, Blues, Black* for National Educational Television.

1970

I Know Why the Caged Bird Sings is published.

1971

Just Give Me a Cool Drink of Water 'fore I Diiie is published.

1974

Gather Together in My Name is published.

1977

Angelou is nominated for an Emmy Award for her portrayal of Kunta Kinte's grandmother in *Roots*.

1981

The Heart of a Woman is published; Angelou accepts a lifetime appointment as a professor at Wake Forest University.

1986

All God's Children Need Traveling Shoes, the fifth volume of Angelou's autobiography, is published.

1993

Angelou reads her poem, "On the Pulse of Morning" at President Bill Clinton's inauguration.

1994

My Painted House, My Friendly Chicken, and Me is published.

2002

The final volume of Angelou's autobiography, *A Song Flung Up to Heaven,* is published.

2004

Angelou's cookbook, *Hallelujah! The Welcome Table*, is published.

2007

Angelou begins working on a libretto for a new opera by Richard Danielpour.

2008

Angelou celebrates her eightieth birthday on April 4.

For More Information

Books

Maya Angelou, *I Know Why the Caged Bird Sings*. New York: Random House, 1969. Very readable, with helpful information on her early life, especially her years in Stamps.

Michael Benson, *Malcolm X*. Minneapolis, MN: Lerner, 2005. Excellent biography of the man who had a huge influence on Maya Angelou and her ideas of civil rights politics.

Kenneth Davis, *Don't Know Much About Martin Luther King, Jr*. New York: HarperCollins, 2006. Good information about the Southern Christian Leadership Conference; helpful index.

L. Patricia Kite, *Maya Angelou*. Minneapolis, MN: Lerner, 2006. Very easy reading; good sidebars connecting various times of Angelou's life with important historical events.

Periodicals

Hillel Italie, "Nearing Her 80th Birthday, Poet Sees Life as Adventure," Charleston (WV) *Sunday Gazette-Mail*, March 30, 2008.

Jim Sparks, "A Unifier of People; A Mixed Crowd Sings, Dances in Celebration," *Winston-Salem* (NC) *Journal*, April 20, 2008.

Clarence Waldron, "Maya Angelou Shares Ways to Celebrate and Express Your Love on Mother's Day," *Jet*, May 7, 2007.

Alice Wyllie, "'The Older I Become the Less I Know,'" *Scotsman* (Edinburgh), April 4, 2008.

Internet Sources

African American Literature Book Club, "Maya Angelou," African American Literature Book Club, http://aalbc.com/authors/maya.htm.

Ken Kelley, "Visions: Maya Angelou," *Mother Jones*, May–June 1995. www.motherjones.com/arts/qa/1995/05/kelley.html.

Web Sites

African Americans.com (www.africanamericans.com). This Web site offers extensive information about African Americans, including slavery, the civil rights movement, black leaders, and African American art and music. The site also provides a history of the song, "African American National Anthem," as well as a biography of its author, James Weldon Johnson.

Dr. Maya Angelou, the Official Website (www.mayaangelou.com). This site offers a complete list of Angelou's accomplishments, awards, and books. It also includes recent news about her activities.

Picture Credits

Cover image: Dave Allocca/DMI/Time Life Pictures/Getty Images
© AISA/Everett Collection, 27
AP Images, 8, 37, 54, 79
© Bettmann/Corbis, 76
© Corbis, 13, 21
Everett Collection, 81
Ben Fink/Jupiterimages, 41
Fotos International/Hulton Archive/Getty Images, 82
© G. Paul Bishop 1954, 59
Image copyright Scott Rothstein, 2009. Used under license
    from Shutterstock.com, 51
Dmitri Kessel/Time Life Pictures/Getty Images, 72
Dorothea Lange/National Archives/Time & Life Pictures/Getty
    Images, 33
Gene Lester/Getty Images, 57
Lipnitzki/Roger Viollet/Getty Images, 67
Brad Markel/Liaison/Getty Images, 7
Plainpicture/K. Ruge/Jupiterimages, 46
Public Domain, 28
Moses Robinson/WireImage/Getty Images, 75
G.W. Romer/Getty Images, 16
© Marc Royce/Corbis, 86
Howard Sochurek/Time Life Pictures/Getty Images, 63
John Vacha/FPG/Getty Images, 15

Gail Stewart is the author of more than 240 books for children and teens. She is the mother of three grown sons, and lives in Minneapolis, Minnesota.